LYNDSIE BARRIE

Collaborators: Liz Campbell, Cynthia Hamilton Urquhart,
Hanna Bracken, Kelly Sinclair, Carey Wilkinson Lee,
Mélanie Higuchi and Stacey Watts.

Photography by Lisa Henry
Cover and interior layout design by Lyndsie Barrie
Edited by Laurie Lakeman, Ute Gilbert and Carey Wilkinson Lee

ISBN 978-0-9953385-2-4 (Paperback)
ISBN 978-0-9953385-3-1 (eBook)

DEDICATION

This book is dedicated to the man who gave me the Hoffman Process.

All proceeds from the sale of this book go into the Fempreneur Foundation, a fund which provides women with leadership, financial and business skill development programs. Beginning in 2020, the fund will pay for at least one woman each year to participate in the Hoffman Process.

Learn more at yycfempreneurs.com/foundation.

CONTENTS

DISCLAIMER

This book is not intended to serve as legal or financial advice. The strategies and concepts contained herein may not be suitable for your situation. Neither the publisher, nor the author shall be liable for any loss of profit or any other commercial damages.

In 2014, I got fired from what I thought was my dream job. It was one of the hardest things I've been through.

It was also one of the greatest blessings of my life.

Like most businesses, mine started from experiencing a problem, solving it, and sharing the solutions with others. That's what you will find in this book: many stories of problems and solutions.

My problems led me to my purpose.

The first problem I experienced, which led me to my purpose, was doubting my ability to become financially secure from doing things I love to do.

While working as a hairdresser at age 21, I decided to quit my job at the salon and start my own mobile hairdressing business. It wasn't my idea.

One of my clients wanted me to do her hair at her house (so she could sip wine and watch soap operas while her colour processed). I asked a few of my other clients what they thought of that idea and they, too, said they were in. So I did it.

That was my first business. For eight years, my mobile hairdressing business provided a flexible schedule and a decent income. The flexible schedule was extremely valuable after I became a mom. Then I became bored. I needed a challenge.

My next problem that led me to my purpose was having very little understanding of how money and business work. I learned how investments work from a hairdressing client when I was 21. He asked me if I wanted to own a salon one day so I could make money without having to trade hours for dollars. I told him it would be my worst nightmare to manage a bunch of hairdressers. (Hairdressers, in my opinion at the time, were not great at teamwork or encouraging one another.) He suggested I look into owning pieces of other people's companies as a way to diversify my income. I took his advice.

Eight years later, I wasn't just bored with my solo-preneur life, I was disappointed. I wanted to do more, but I wasn't clear on what "more" looked like. After reading a couple of books about money and investing, I was angry that my school teachers and parents forgot to include the money, business and investing lessons. Although I was still interested in the world of beauty and I loved doing hair, I had known for years that my purpose was bigger than that. My problem was comfort. I was scared to leave my comfort zone.

I finally worked up the courage to put my house up for sale and found a way to make a new start in Cochrane, Alberta. Many times I thought about applying at a bank, but I didn't want to put my young son in childcare and I didn't want a boss or a bunch of co-workers, in case they were not friendly. Also, I was afraid of rejection. I didn't think they'd hire a hairdresser to work with people's money (WRONG!).

I found a part-time job at a medi-spa downtown Calgary and secured a spot for my son at a day home in Cochrane. I quickly realized I was barely breaking even on this deal. In time, I made a connection that would get me into a financial advisor training program.

One day at the medi-spa, one of the clients and I started chatting. It turned out she lived a block away from me in Cochrane! That connection started me on the path that led me to my purpose.

Fast-forward past many grueling financial courses, exams and one very long hiring process, I began working as a financial advisor for a large international investment firm. I had a fancy office, an assistant, and a growing group of (mostly) lovely clients. Unfortunately, the client list wasn't growing fast enough to keep me hitting the commission targets.

Three years later, I was fired.

After sobbing for about a day, I started to see the silver lining: this was meant to happen. I wasn't meant to work for that company. I was supposed to start my own business where I would no longer be a salesperson with a phoney, deceiving title: "Financial Advisor". I would finally get to do what I knew I was supposed to do: teach people all the important money, business and investing stuff we didn't learn in school.

Most of my clients from the investment firm (all of the loveliest ones) came with me when I started my own financial consulting company in 2014 because there was one thing I was great at, thanks to my many years as a hairdresser:

Meaningful Conversations.

The clients I had built the strongest relationships with were going wherever I went.

Although the investment firm had let me go for not earning enough commissions, when my clients moved their money into the new investments on my "product shelf", my income was higher than before! I was in shock the first few months as I saw the dollars going into my bank account. I couldn't believe my clients were paying lower fees and I was making more money because I no longer had the prestigious office and assistant - the "dream job" I so desperately wanted months before! Sometimes I still think back to moving my stuff out of my office, sobbing, wondering if I had failed, if I would have to admit defeat and walk away from all those relationships and promises I'd made to serve those people. That feeling - the uncertainty and lack of confidence - SUCKED.

Another feeling that sucked was feeling alone. Loneliness and a lack of accountability were two of my greatest problems as I built my business. My desire to help you build your own supportive community is the key reason why I'm writing this book.

When I decided to move 800kms away from my family to start a new life, I missed them for the first few years. Although I hadn't lived in my home town for many years, I had been only an hour and a half drive away. I knew I needed to build a new support network, and over time, the right people came along. It was tough, opening myself up to people who might not be trustworthy. I had my heart broken a few times. I felt rejected a few times. I made mistakes and realized how to be a better friend in future situations.

As I struggled to build my business and my community, my mom, who of course only wanted what was best for me, suggested that I just "go get a job". She wanted me to stop fighting so hard to be my own boss and take what she thought was the easy route:

Get a job.
(??!!??!!??)

Have you been there?

Have you felt like no one gets what you're trying to do, what you feel called to do?

It's so hard to push through not only others' doubt, but also those moments when you doubt yourself. Looking back on the many times when negative feelings were trying to take hold of me, I am proud of the way I persevered. I am so damn proud of myself for how I responded to the voices in my head telling me I would probably be broke forever: by working harder, living leaner (budget-wise) and continuing to build my team and serve my clients.

My faith and perseverance paid off: I didn't stay broke forever. I hired a business coach and wrote my first book, a process that taught me tons about who I am, what I believe and who I want to serve. I focused less on thinking of myself and what I wanted and more on how I can help others. Naturally, those messages came out in my social media posts. I began attracting the right teammates and clients.

Although I had read about others' mindset shifts in books and heard stories on podcasts and Ted Talks, my life changing mindset shifts didn't begin until November 2018 during something called the "Hoffman Process".

One week.

26 strangers.

Re-living childhood experiences.

Imagining conversations with loved ones.

Sharing deep, dark secrets, hopes and dreams.

Sobbing.

Seeing my future - the bright one.

Seeing my future - the wrong one.

Saying "I love you" to people who were strangers only days before.

For one week, I followed instructions to re-route my brain's neuropathways. I saw what I needed to do to make my bright future become reality: loving, supportive people. I saw how a group of strangers with a common goal can become a family to one another. I felt the connection that happens when a group of people share their stories, hopes and challenges. I also felt disconnection, more like rejection, when one of our "Hoffmates" chose to leave us on the third day, saying it wasn't for her. Timing is everything. It wasn't her time.

The Hoffman Process was given to me and all the other people I experienced it with. It was the perfect gift at the perfect time in my life. Had I not received that gift from a generous, kind soul, you would not be reading this book.

The one thing the giver asked each of us to do was simply, *"Pay it forward."*

During my Hoffman Process, I envisioned a group of women, a community. I saw them gaining confidence in their ability to become financially secure from doing things they love to do. I watched them finding their voices on social media. These visions excited me. Admittedly, my excitement was also a bit selfish. I wanted to have a family of women around me who are excited about the same stuff I get excited about!!!

I knew I wanted to start some sort of free marketing school for women, a way for me to share the solutions I found to my problems as I built my business.

Although the Hoffman Process helped me become more loving, it didn't cure my fear of gathering a group of women. The memories of high school friend drama and working in the salon still haunted me, but they became less and less scary the harder I focused on my vision, my free marketing school and supportive community of women. Ultimately, I came away from the Hoffman Process with more trust in myself than I had ever had before.

Hopefully by the time you read this, I will have passed the 100 mark - 100 women who have gained knowledge and confidence from my free marketing school or from reading and completing the action steps in this book.

It is an incredible feeling to be surrounded by women who are getting outside their comfort zones to do big, bold things, including sharing their important messages and stories on social media. This is the environment I work hard to provide for women in my free six week marketing school, which is called "Fempreneur Marketing School". This is also the environment I'll show you how to create for yourself in this book.

NOTE: If the word "marketing" terrifies or confuses you, *THIS BOOK WAS WRITTEN FOR YOU!*

These pages contain a six week process that builds confidence and clarity in women, especially women who own a business or who want to get their business idea off the ground. Each week, I'll share one of the six foundational marketing principles that revealed themselves to me as I fought to create my purpose-based business.

This book is a true testament to the power of a like-minded team. This book was created by a team of women who are passionate about supporting other women: Mélanie Higuchi, Cynthia Hamilton Urquhart, Liz Campbell, Carey Wilkinson Lee, Stacey Watts, Hanna Bracken, and Kelly Sinclair, thank you all so much for getting behind this book project by sharing your stories, ideas and valuable feedback. Most of all, your friendship means the world to me.

The next person I want to thank is my son. He is my number one accountability partner, favourite hockey player, best camping buddy and the most valuable gift God will ever give me.

If you are someone reading this who I haven't met yet, it is my sincere hope that we will become friends. Before you dive into chapter one, please send me a Facebook message or email and let me know what you hope to learn or improve over the next six weeks! Thank you!

Facebook.com/lyndsie.barrie
Instagram.com/yycfempreneurs
Email: lyndsie@yycfempreneurs.com

Thank you for reading this book! I look forward to getting to know you!

Lyndsie Barrie

Relationships make or break every single organization. It's true: culture is key. "Culture" is a common word among employees and business owners alike because it comes from the Latin word *cultura*, which means to grow or cultivate. The best way to cultivate a garden applies to growing a dream team of like-minded women: **SHOW YOU CARE.**

The reason why showing you care is more effective than simply being the expert is people won't care how much you know until they know how much you care.

People won't care how much you know until they know how much you care.

When my free six week marketing school launched in February 2019, my focus was on building relationships first. Creating a welcoming, safe environment was my number one goal and number two was building the lesson material. There were growing pains, missing instructions and total confusion at times, but one thing was crystal clear to all the women based on the feedback I received over and over again: *Lyndsie cares deeply about helping us succeed.*

I care about you and because I care, I will remind you often to build and maintain relationships with other women who are doing big, bold things. These women are your dream team. Without a dream team supporting you, this book will have zero impact on your life. If you don't use this book as a tool to create a team of ladies who will encourage you and celebrate with you, this book will not help you. In fact, I suspect this book will frustrate you and cause you to feel overwhelmed if you try to put it into action on your own.

Meet my friend Carey Wilkinson Lee...

Recently, in a BIG, white, stumbling burst of clarity, I discovered that I've been having an abusive relationship with myself.

After 30+ years of struggling, searching and bumbling about, I was happy to have finally labeled my (seeming life-long) condition. I was feeling relief and clarity but I was also overcome by the feeling of fear. What now? I couldn't just pack up the car and drive away from my low self-esteem!

It has been an exhausting journey leading up to this realization, but along the way, I have learned a lot of simple yet amazing tricks. Over the course of a few years, I have shared some of these tricks with a few like-minded, inspiring women in my life who I respect and admire. My amazing tribe of girls almost had me convinced that I should share my struggles and tricks to help others. They encouraged me to get it all out of my head, written down and organized. They told me to write a book!

A book?! You must be joking!!

But these beautiful friends had planted a seed. When I was alone and let myself dream, the thought of writing my own book made me giddy. The idea that I could have a book with my name on it felt right. The process and the way I would feel after completion, holding the final product in my hands, gifting it to my mom and dad ignited extreme excitement in my soul!

As I settled into my intention to write a book, I realized that I had a big problem: organizing my thoughts and setting aside time to write wasn't happening.

When I even thought about starting, my brain and body froze. I felt like Han Solo - frozen in carbonite! I had written notes in several notebooks all over my house, recorded voice clips on several devices, emailed images, quotes and inspirational sayings to myself, but I had no idea how to make myself actually start the process of writing a book. I was labelling the feeling as "completely overwhelmed", when, in fact, there was a fair bit of laziness and definitely some procrastination to blame for my lack of action.

Still, I really wanted to write a book.

What I know: There is a solution to every problem.

I also know that finding out exactly what the problem is can be extremely difficult, especially without help.

The first thing I did was make it a priority to solve the problem: "how to get the knowledge out of my head and into a book?"

The second thing I did was enlist the help of my tribe of girls, who had fantastic suggestions of how to get out of my own way.

As I pondered their suggestions, it hit me, a scary yet inspiring realization: I had to become a different person. I had to change my daily routine and habits into that of a person on a mission.

To write this book, I had to:

- *Stop making excuses*

- *Drink less alcohol*

- *Get around motivated and inspiring women more often*

- *Embrace my ADHD brain and be proud of who I am*

- *Believe that I am a writer*

- *Trust that sharing my stories will help others*

- *Tell my friends and family I'm writing a book*

The last step was hard for me, which I did in a Facebook live video!!

Although I had told many people I was writing a book, I had no actual words written. That's when I took ACTION!

First, I decided to put down Candy Crush. This WAS NOT easy.

Second, I had to stop Googling the "British Royals".

Next, I decided to use binge watching Suits as a reward for getting writing done. I stopped picking up historical fiction books at second-hand stores. I made regular appointments with a therapist. I researched the ADHD brain and how I could harness my creativity. None of this was easy. I had a really hard time getting started writing my book.

I was doing a better job of creating mental space to write, but I just couldn't write. I tried writing on the couch, at the kitchen table, in my back yard, at coffee shops - not working. I couldn't get started writing. I kept thinking, "if only I had a house with a view or a cottage I could escape to. THEN, I would start." … I had a lot of excuses.

I knew there was a solution to this problem, it just took me a lot longer than I'd hoped it would to find it.

Finally, it hit me - like a BIG, white, stumbling burst of clarity!

It was too simple and I was actually a little embarrassed that this was what took me so long to start writing. It was the answer though - my whole body knew it was true when I said it.

I hadn't found a creative space!

The truth is, I had always known where it was, I just wouldn't admit it because it wasn't a "normal" writing space.

After I figured it out, I got settled with my laptop on my lap and my dog snuggled beside me…

In my BED!

Since figuring out where I love to write, I've gotten to work at writing a weekly blog post focused on mental health. This writing will soon become my book, called "How to Stop Having An Abusive Relationship with Yourself."

When you can't find the solution to a problem, get help. And if you need some tactical ways to get out of your own way, I have some great information waiting for you in my blog at careywilkinsonlee.com!

**"When you can't find the solution to a problem, get help."
-Carey Wilkinson Lee**

It takes courage to share your message with the world. This book alone will not give you courage. You must combine the information in this book with a team of women who are in the trenches with you, working alongside you to achieve your common goals.

Gather a team of like-minded ladies who will cheer you on and brainstorm with you.

In order to have a team backing you, you need to be a team player. This means the relationships you build must be mutually beneficial in order for them to last longer than a few months. You want them to share what's working for them, so share your great ideas and plans with them. You want them to give you feedback on your latest blog post or video, so remember to include your offer to help them in your request for help.

You gotta give to get.

It's time for you to be a leader, even if you've never been a leader before. You need a team, and there are women out there who need you to lead them to finding their voice on social media. This book is designed to help you gather a group of 3-5 women alongside you. All you need to do is follow the education system I created, Fempreneur Marketing School, in this book and trust me when I tell you that *your commitment to yourself and your team will reap huge benefits - more than you can imagine.*

Here's what you say to that voice in your head that is telling you you're not a leader or that leading a group of women will be awful:

I love to support other women. I trust Lyndsie's proven system to guide me in leading this course. I want to surround myself with a team of women who are working to become more confident and fulfilled! It's a win-win!

If you had a negative experience working with a group of women in the past, listen to Episode 3 of the Fempreneur Marketing Podcast, "Thanks for firing me" for encouragement and leadership advice. You can find this and all episodes at fempreneurmarketing.com/podcast.

You will create a safe, caring community of like-minded women. I'll help you. Building a community starts with meaningful conversation, and meaningful conversations start with asking great questions. I'm going to walk you through what to say and be by your side every step of the way!

Here's how you will invite 3-5 women to join you if you are willing and able to lead a group…

☐ LEADER ACTION STEP #1:
INVITATION SCRIPT

If you are willing and able to lead a group of ladies through the lessons and action steps in this book, send this email/message to 5 women now (you want an even number of teammates because you will partner up):

"Would you like to join me in taking a free six week course to learn new ways to…

(Insert the best option for her situation:)

- *build your brand and share your clear message on social media?"*

- *find your voice on social media?"*

(Next paragraph:)

"The lesson material is in a book I just started reading and one of the first things the book recommends is gathering a team of like-minded ladies, which made me think of you. The time commitment each week is a one hour virtual meeting with the group plus four hours for completing the action steps provided. Would you like to join me in taking this free course?"

Ladies who are interested will respond with questions about what they will learn and meeting logistics. For course info, send them to fempreneurmarketing.com to read the testimonials and do their research. To nail down a weekly meeting time for 6 weeks, provide 2 times that will work for you and once your first teammate has committed to a time, offer only that time to the rest of the women you invite. I recommend you have no more than 6 women on your team including you. *(Reminder: you want an even number as you will partner up.)*

As soon as you send your invitation emails, let me know you have taken the first step towards finding your voice on social media using one of the following links to YYC Fempreneurs on Facebook or Instagram:

facebook.com/yycfempreneurs
instagram.com/yycfempreneurs

NOTE: If you don't have Facebook or Instagram yet, now is the time to set up your accounts!

Once you're on Facebook or Instagram @yycfempreneurs, pick one of the recent posts and add a comment. Type something like:

"Hello! I've just started reading the Find Your Voice book and I have committed to leading a group of women through Fempreneur Marketing School!"

A sentence describing your biggest takeaway from the book so far would be great to see, too! If you need more members to join your team, you are welcome to invite other women reading your post to get in touch with you to join!

From Experiment to Procedure

In February 2019, before we met for Session One of Fempreneur Marketing School, my first group of ladies were chatting away, getting to know each other in our group chat. The conversation started flowing after I asked each woman to record and share an intro video in our group chat. Every part of that first group was experimental, but the intro video quickly proved to be a fundamental part of my Fempreneur Marketing School process because doing that one thing, a simple video (which took some women fifty attempts before they felt good enough to share it), smashed through many creativity and confidence blocks right off the bat. They also saw within the first few days of being part of this new community of women, that there are many others facing the same challenges and lacking confidence in the same areas. The videos also jump-started the trust building process between the women.

Throughout this book, you're going to get to know many Fempreneur Marketing School Grads by reading their stories. These are real women who you can reach out to directly on Facebook, Instagram or through their websites with questions or simply to let them know how their stories have impacted your life. By the end of the book, they, like me, will be part of your Fempreneur Community. Once you complete this book, you will be asked to share your experience with me, and, with your permission, I will feature your story on the YYC Fempreneurs social channels and the Fempreneur Marketing Podcast to connect you with even more like-minded women!

As you noticed from flipping through this book, there are many pages where you are encouraged to record your answers to the questions, goals and To-Do lists. There may not be enough room here for what you want to write so *always have a pen and notebook handy*. And not just any notebook - one notebook - the same notebook every time. I've never been successful at having 2 or 3 notebooks, one for personal stuff and one for business, for example. IT DOES NOT WORK. Stick to one notebook for all things and keep it like a journal, in chronological order. Keep everything in there. Client notes. Ideas. Prayers. Stories. All of it.

NOTE: If you have <u>not</u> committed to leading a group through Fempreneur Marketing School, you can skip ahead to the next chapter, although <u>I do not recommend this!</u>

☐ LEADER ACTION STEP #2:
LEADER PORTAL

Thank you for committing to your role as a Fempreneur Marketing School Leader! Building a team of like-minded ladies who will support you and lean on you for support will be one of the most rewarding things you ever do, and I'd be willing to bet this won't be the only time you'll lead this course!

Once you have an even number of ladies committed, register your group at fempreneurmarketing.com/leaders. Once you are registered, you will receive an email with a link to access the Fempreneur Leader Portal.

☐ LEADER ACTION STEP #3:
TEAM VALUES & COMMITMENT

Read and email to your teammates the *Fempreneur Vision and Commitment* descriptions (next page and in leader portal). Ask them to respond confirming they have read and agree with the Fempreneur Vision and Commitment. Their response is their entrance into your team's Facebook Group Chat where much of the marketing and accountability magic will happen!

NOTE: The Fempreneur Vision and Commitment descriptions can be found when you login to the Fempreneur Leader Portal. From there, you can copy them from the PDF and paste them into an email to your team. (If you don't know how to copy and paste text on your computer, Google it.)

FEMPRENEUR TEAM VALUES

Read and <u>initial</u> next to each of the value statements:

- We offer and accept support, encouragement and honest feedback, always assuming criticism is coming from a place of love.

- We try new things and take risks.

- We find answers to business and marketing questions through research and share our findings openly with our teammates.

- We create structure and firm boundaries around family time, me time and business time.

- We never discuss another member's personal or confidential business information outside this community. Everything shared here stays here.

- We never approach another member of this community to sell to her. Instead of focusing on short term financial gain, we strive to develop long-lasting friendships and team spirit.

FEMPRENEUR TEAM COMMITMENT

Before emailing these commitments to your team, fill in the blanks and initial next to each commitment:

1. *I will attend six weekly group sessions on Zoom from ___am/pm - ___am/pm beginning on _____, 20___.*

2. *I will schedule and attend six weekly meetings with my partner (virtual or in person.)*

3. *I will invest four hours of focused time in my business every week to complete the action steps described in the "Find Your Voice" book.*

4. *I will send a private message to each member of my team offering support and encouragement at least once each week.*

Once all teammates have responded to the email confirming they are on-board, it's time to connect your team!

☐ LEADER ACTION STEP #4:

FACEBOOK GROUP CHAT

Ensuring you are Facebook friends with all your teammates, connect your team in a Facebook group chat.

The relationships are what 80% of Fempreneur Grads say were their most valuable take away from Fempreneur Marketing School.

Your Facebook group chat will be where most of the relationship building magic happens!

If you don't know how to start a Facebook group chat, *Google it*. Most of what I'm going to teach you in this book I learned from searching my question at google.com. ***Reminder to ensure the instructions you are following are recent!*

NOTE: I will not be sharing technology instructions here in the book because technology is always changing. You will, however, find up to date how-to videos and step-by-step instructions online at:

fempreneurmarketing.com/week1 - Purpose

fempreneurmarketing.com/week2 - Conversation

fempreneurmarketing.com/week3 - Service

fempreneurmarketing.com/week4 - Storytelling

fempreneurmarketing.com/week5 - Create

fempreneurmarketing.com/week6 - Automate

If you can't find what you need at any of those links, you know what to do (google.com)!

☐ LEADER ACTION STEP #5:
INTRO VIDEOS

Get the conversation flowing by recording a welcome video of yourself saying something like:

"Welcome Fempreneurs! I'm so excited to lead you through six weeks of marketing education and team building! So we can all learn about one another, please post a video here in the chat introducing yourself, what you love about your business and why you decided to join us. I'll go first..."

Share your answers in your video. Try to keep the video shorter than 2 minutes to avoid having to chop it into 2 videos and post it/them in the chat. Over the next 7-10 days, keep positive conversation flowing in your Facebook Group Chat.

I'd love to be able to welcome you and your team to Fempreneur Marketing School, so please send me a Facebook friend request, if you haven't already, (Lyndsie Barrie) and invite me to join your Group Chat too! I'd love to welcome everyone and get to know all of you by watching your intro videos!

A note about Negative Nancy.

If a member of your team is using the group chat as a place to vent her negative thoughts and feelings, do your best to put a positive spin on it or do what I do - quickly change the subject to something positive. Ask her a question that cannot be turned negative, like *"What are you most excited to learn or improve over the next 6 weeks?"* If Negative Nancy responds with something like, *"Nothing at the moment. I'm hoping I can learn how to love my business again over the next 6 weeks"*, here's what I'd do: I would send her a private message asking for her phone number and a good time to call. I'd ask her the question which will be coming in Session One: *"What is one skill you are committed to learning or improving during the Fempreneur Marketing Course?"* If she comes back with something negative and you are getting the feeling she is going to be more work than you want to take on, or that she will likely drag the rest of the group down, politely ask her to leave. Tell her you want what's best for the group and you feel she is in need of a level of support you are not able to provide. Blame your lack of leadership experience, *"It's not you, it's me..."*

If you are an extremely empathetic person or maybe just much nicer than I am, what you just read may sound mean, but I stand by what I said. You need to be cautious of giving the impression that the Fempreneur Marketing School is for anyone and everyone, because it is not. The key trait that must be present in every member of your team is that they _care_ about each other and want to _support_ their team. Negative Nancys have dug themselves into a deep hole filled with negativity. Throw her a rope, but if she doesn't use it to climb out and instead seems to be trying to pull you and others down, walk away. Once relationships are built, some negativity or self doubt can be handled and worked through as a group, but in my experience, someone who comes into a new group with nothing but negative stuff to say requires a level of help and support you can't provide.

☐ LEADER ACTION STEP #6:
PREPARE FOR SESSION ONE

A few days before Session One, review the Session One Leader Guide in the Fempreneur Leader Portal (instructions are in the email you received when you registered your team).

As a member of the Fempreneur Leadership Team, you will receive lots of helpful FREE coaching along the way in the form of videos, checklists and invitations to live in-person and online training!

Thanks in advance for taking the leader survey during week three of Fempreneur Marketing School. I'm looking forward to learning from you how I can improve the leader material!

DREAM TEAM
Chapter Summary

- The best way to build a team of like-minded women is to SHOW YOU CARE.

- You will get minimum impact from this book if you don't do the work alongside a team.

- 85% percent of the women surveyed said the most valuable thing they gained from Fempreneur Marketing School was A SUPPORTIVE TEAM.

- If you don't have Facebook or Instagram yet, now is the time to set up your accounts.

- Your team's Facebook group chat is where you will keep your teammates connected.

- If you don't know how to do something, GOOGLE IT!

- Please connect with me on Facebook so I can welcome you and your teammates to Fempreneur Marketing School!

- *"When you can't find the solution to a problem, get help."* -Carey Wilkinson Lee

People are often shocked that my six week marketing school is free. They can't believe I give away that much of my time and knowledge. No matter who tells me to charge money for it, no matter how smart and accomplished they are, I will say no.

It's easy to find your voice and put yourself out there to the world when you have a clear vision of what success looks like. I know that my marketing school has to involve zero financial risk for women, otherwise it would not be in line with my purpose.

My purpose is to help as many women as possible feel financially secure through creating profitable, purposeful businesses.

In this chapter, you're going to get closer to identifying your purpose so you can confidently share it, whether on social media, from stage, in your own book, or across the table from your clients.

Whether you're a hairstylist, stock broker, dog trainer, seamstress or karate instructor,

Marketing is Simply Building Relationships.

After I got fired and started my own business, I appreciated the freedom to build relationships my way. When I was working for the investment firm, I had to abide by their marketing guidelines. I wasn't allowed to post on social media about my financial workshops or ANYTHING to do with the world of finance or investing without their permission. In order to work for the firm, I had to give them permission to see everything I posted on Facebook (at the time, that was my only social media account). I felt like they owned me.

As I built my financial consulting business, I met new financial product reps. A few of them offered to hold live events where they provided the space and refreshments and I brought the people. A small community formed as I began to hold these events on a bi-monthly basis. I advertised these events as a way to network (first and foremost), with a small mention of the financial product pitch that would also happen. Not only did people make connections, but I also gained new clients. More clients meant more income, but the money didn't mask what I knew in my heart: my business still wasn't in line with my purpose.

About a year after I started my financial consulting business, I attended a financial industry conference. The keynote speaker seemed to have built the career I was trying to build: a three-time author, a "Financial Advisor" with strong connections in the philanthropy world and a respected educator on how to make the most impact with charitable donations. From the stage, he told his life story then wrapped up with a pitch to help financial professionals grow their businesses and **write a book**. A few months later, I hired him because what he said on stage made sense, and still does today:

You have a moral obligation to share what you know.

I thought back to the reason why I first decided to pursue a career in finance. It was because I grew up knowing very little about money, investing, starting a business, taxes - all the financial things. This frustrated me and I wanted to do something about it. I thought, *"If I can get paid to learn about stuff I've always wanted to learn and then get paid to share it with others, why the heck would I do anything else?"*

That powerful statement, "You have a moral obligation to share what you know", lit a fire in my soul.

"Heck, yes I do, buddy! Thanks for reminding me!" I thought. To this very day I'm so grateful he stood on that stage in front of me to remind me what my purpose is. I had been wandering in a different direction and needed a course correction.

It took three months to get in touch with him and let him know I wanted to hire him because I was already stretched financially. When I finally met with him, I opened the conversation confessing that I was a single mom struggling to get my business off the ground and I had no idea how I would afford to pay him, but I needed to learn how to do what he was doing - making a living from teaching, selling books, speaking - not just from selling financial products. He agreed to help me for half his usual fee on a four month contract. I was thrilled. I told him I'd get back to him the next day.

As I drove away, I called my friend Yvonne and told her the details of the meeting. She told me I needed to do it and she felt strongly that I would be happy with my decision to hire him. She said, *"Just trust that you'll find the money."* This did not make sense to me, as someone who advised her clients to plan ahead and save for purchases, but the undeniable feeling that this was what I was supposed to do gave me the confidence to take a leap of faith.

That evening, I checked my credit card balances and found that one of my cards had just enough room to pay for my first month of coaching. I emailed my new business coach telling him I was ready to start.

My business coach shared his purpose in a clear, authentic way with the right people and taught me how to do the same. The lessons I learned from him and many other mentors have enabled me to build income streams from sharing my knowledge. Although my marketing school is free, it feeds many other income streams. It's incredible what happens when you see your purpose clearly and do the work required to have an impact!

Meet my friend Kelly Sinclair...

Lyndsie witnessed me having a big "Aha!" moment as I shared with her the story you are about to read. I was so caught up in motherhood and coping with big life changes that I hadn't realized how pivotal the story I am about to tell you was for me. As I shared this story with Lyndsie at my kitchen table, both of us wiping away tears, I thought, "I need to get over my fears and share this experience that could resonate with other people!" From that moment, I actually had to work really hard to peel back the layers to get to where this all started and find the other missing pieces. I hope my story will help you discover a whole new realm of strength and wisdom inside yourself.

After my second maternity leave, I had gone back to work at the public relations agency I had been working at for six years. We had moved from Calgary to Cochrane which meant I now had a longer commute to get to work downtown Calgary. My husband and I were hauling kids out of bed to get them to the dayhome at 6am. I literally had a THERMOS of coffee and I would be refilling my coffee on the commute, lying to myself thinking, "This is fine. It's just hard to adjust."

In reality, this was not aligned with my definition of success.

As a mother, when you leave your kids behind, your job now has to hold that much more value to you. The value I placed on the work I was doing wasn't even coming close to the value of my role as a mother. But I also knew that working played an important part in my life to help me feel balanced.

As all of this was going on, my mom, who I loved deeply, was battling breast cancer and it took a turn for the worse.

So I made a decision: I would leave my job to spend more time with her.

She passed away eight days later.

I had never experienced loss before. I had all this emotion and grief, but also time and space to reflect on what is really important. I gained a new perspective on life: that it truly is short, so why spend it doing something that doesn't bring you joy? It became crystal clear that I have to be connected to the people and causes that are important to me and truly enjoy the work I do because we spend a third of our lives working.

I decided, in that phase of grief and time after my mom passed, I wanted to take all my communications education and public relations expertise and start my own business. I wanted to help entrepreneurs live their dreams and see their passions be successful through teaching them marketing.

As I uncovered the story of the WHY behind my business and identified my purpose, I created a formula to help other people figure it out, too. My next step was aligning my business with helping people connect with their purpose.

When it comes to connecting with like-minded people, the power of authenticity is huge. Even though I knew this, it was too uncomfortable for me. I thought that if I talked about my mom passing away, people would think I wanted attention or sympathy. As Lyndsie and I talked this through at my kitchen table that day, I realized I had to stop worrying about what others might think and share my story.

The truth is, sharing a personal story isn't selfish. It actually causes people to think about their own stories and how they relate to you. It encourages connection and builds trust.

"Find the courage to be vulnerable and share your stories by getting around women who are boldly sharing their stories."

- Kelly Sinclair

Isn't it great that Kelly and others are willing to share their stories? If you think your story won't have an impact on people, you need to remember all the stories you've heard that have changed your perspective for the better and helped you see things you were missing.

Every woman has a moral obligation to share what she know!

That said, you will run into road blocks along the way to identifying and clearly communicating your message. The action steps in this chapter will help you get ready for the challenges that lie ahead and gather ammo to fight back!

In a moment, I'm going to ask you to write one skill you are committed to learning or improving in the next six weeks. First, let's look at some common answers women have shared in Fempreneur Marketing School:

- Get better at putting out on social media what it is that I do in an attractive way.

- Actually make time for my business outside of my 9-5 job.

- Learn how to build an engaged community on Facebook (in preparation to launch my online store.)

- Make new connections in my new industry on social media and at live events.

- Get more comfortable with posting videos of myself on social media.

- Clarify who my ideal client is so I can market specifically to them.

☐ ACTION STEP #1

Get out your notebook or use the space provided in the book to write your answers:

1. What is one skill you are committed to learning or improving over the next 6 weeks?

2. *If you won a $100,000 cash prize or inheritance today, what would you do tomorrow? How is that different than what you will actually do tomorrow?*

3. *If the amount of your cash prize or inheritance was $1,000,000, how would your life and business look different tomorrow?*

4. *Describe the career and philanthropic (giving back) success you desire.*

5. What's holding you back from achieving your definition of success?

☐ ACTION STEP #2

Schedule six weekly meetings with your Fempreneur partner.

***Fempreneur Leaders will assign partners during the first group training session, which I recommend is held virtually on Zoom (zoom.us). If you are not part of a group, make sure you have someone to work with over the next six weeks!

Aim to have your first partner meeting ASAP after reading this chapter.

☐ ACTION STEP #3

This is the agenda for your first meeting with your partner:

1. Ask your partner to share her answers from Action Step #1. When you get to the fifth question, "What's holding you back from achieving your definition of success?", write **SMASH LIST** at the top of a blank page in your notebooks (or use page 50 in this book). Take turns

brainstorming specific, measurable goals that will help you **smash through the roadblocks** you wrote down.

2. Each of you will write 3-5 specific, measurable goals on your *SMASH LIST.*

3. Take turns helping each other choose one goal from your *SMASH LIST* which you are committed to achieving in the next 2-3 weeks.

4. Ask your partner how you can help her achieve that goal and write what she says here:

SMASH LIST

☐ ACTION STEP #4

Get a goal board and draw six boxes on it, like this:

My Goals

Week 1	Week 3	Week 5
Week 2	Week 4	Week 6

Write the goal you committed to achieving in the next 2-3 weeks in the week 1 box.

You're serious about setting and achieving goals, right?

It's time to get to work smashing through your roadblocks!

Although writing down goals on paper is proven to help you achieve them, you also need the right mindset. You need to be clear on WHY you want to achieve your goals. This next exercise will help you do exactly that.

To help you continue to clarify your purpose, or your WHY, you're going to write 5-10 of the most valuable lessons you've learned from books, podcasts, mentors, and problems you had to solve.

For example, the problems I faced as I built my business became the six lessons in Fempreneur Marketing School (next page…).

PROBLEM:

I was going it alone.
I didn't have a team.
I felt like no one understood my struggles.

FEMPRENEUR MARKETING SCHOOL WEEK ONE:

PROBLEM:

I didn't know how to post on social media in a way that would attract my ideal clients.

FEMPRENEUR MARKETING SCHOOL WEEK TWO:

PROBLEM:

"Fake it 'til you make it!" was my motto. I thought asking my clients what they needed help with made me seem like I didn't know what I was doing.

FEMPRENEUR MARKETING SCHOOL WEEK THREE:

PROBLEM:

"Be vulnerable with someone other than a therapist who is sworn to confidentiality? No thanks!" I didn't realize how important it is to share my WHY message.

FEMPRENEUR MARKETING SCHOOL WEEK FOUR:

PROBLEM:

I thought I needed expensive graphic design programs to create eye-catching images and marketing materials.

FEMPRENEUR MARKETING SCHOOL WEEK FIVE:

PROBLEM:

The ability to plan and schedule my social media posts didn't exist!

FEMPRENEUR MARKETING SCHOOL WEEK SIX:

☐ ACTION STEP #5

Write 5-10 of the most valuable lessons you've learned from books, podcasts, mentors, and problems you had to solve. List the source of the lesson and how it improved your life for the better. Put stars beside the events/lessons that led you to realizing your purpose.

SHOW OFF YOUR SUCCESS!

Once you've completed all the action steps from this week and met with your partner, print and add the TEAM BADGE to your goal board! Find it at fempreneurmarketing.com/week1.

1.
PURPOSE
Chapter Summary

- Marketing is simply building relationships

- You have a moral obligation to share what you know.

- Keep building your dream team one authentic, inspiring woman at a time!

- Take the time to paint your picture of career and philanthropic (giving back) success.

- In order to achieve your goals, you must meet with your partner each week and complete the action steps provided! (The book doesn't work if you don't!)

- You need to be clear on WHY you want to achieve your goals.

- Reflecting on the life events and mentors who have had the greatest impact on your life will help you discover or clarify your purpose.

- *"Find the courage to be vulnerable and share your stories by getting around women who are boldly sharing their stories."*
  - Kelly Sinclair

When I began working with my business coach, I valued my skills and knowledge on a scale of 1-10. I rated myself at a 2 or 3 and famous authors and finance gurus on BNN at 9 or 10.

I was looking at it all wrong.

The number one reason why the money I invested in hiring a business coach paid me HUGE returns is my coach taught me *how to measure the value of my skills and knowledge the RIGHT way* - the way people actually assign value to products and services, by asking themselves two simple questions:

1. *Can she help me solve my problem? Y/N*

If someone reading or watching your post on social media can answer *Yes* to that question, what do you think they will ask next?

BINGO!

2.   *Do I like her? Y/N*

If you don't make it perfectly clear in your marketing that you care about solving their problem, the people you want to serve will move on and forget about you.

Marketing is just conversation.

These two questions, *"Can she help me?"* and, *"Do I like her?"* are not only key in marketing, but are also at the root of every conversation we have with a new person face to face. When getting to know a new person, we ask ourselves, *"What can I get out of this person?"*

I know that sounds… selfish. Maybe even greedy. But it's true!

In my case, what I'm looking for is fun and interesting people. I love to laugh and learn about others' lives, so if someone I'm meeting for the first time is making me laugh, for whatever reason, and has interesting stories to share, my answer to the first question, "What can I get out of this person?", is: FUN, LAUGHTER AND ENTERTAINMENT!

To answer my next question, *"Do I like this new person?"*, I'm watching for things like trustworthiness, honesty, kindness, and common interests.

The trickiest things about using social media as a way to connect with people are:

Your post is floating in a sea of thousands of other posts.
People are busy.

I've seen all sorts of stats on how quickly the human brain answers those two important questions, *"Can she help me? Do I like her?"*. Does it matter if it is 7, 8 or 9 seconds? Maybe. For now, let's assume it is nine seconds and move on to the important question we are going to cover in this chapter:

How are you going to start a meaningful conversation in nine seconds or less on social media?

Before you can effectively communicate the value you have to offer, you must BELIEVE in yourself. You need to own your skills and talents, or as I say most often, OWN YOUR PURPOSE.

☐ ACTION STEP #1

Right now, I want you to stand in front of a mirror, straight and tall (your best Superwoman stance) look yourself in the eyes and say this out loud:

"MY SKILLS AND KNOWLEDGE ARE VALUABLE. I CAN HELP PEOPLE LIVE BETTER LIVES BY SHARING MY KNOWLEDGE WITH THEM."

Write how that made you feel in the space below. If you aren't sure, say it out loud again and again until you can find the words to describe the emotions you feel.

If you're having trouble finding the words, see if there are any words on this list that describe how you felt when declaring the value you have to offer:

Alert	Apprehensive
Stimulated	Worried
Excited	Frustrated
Inspired	Confused
Confident	Disconnected
Radiant	Distracted
Comfortable	Alarmed
Calm	Ashamed
Renewed	Self-conscious
Loving	Exhausted
Empathetic	Hopeless
Surprised	Insecure

If you are doubting the value you have to offer, here is your reality check and confidence boost:

You don't have to be <u>the</u> expert to improve lives.

You don't have to know it all to help solve people's problems. Whether you realize it or not, you are AN EXPERT and your knowledge combined with your unique life experiences are VALUABLE!

YOUR KNOWLEDGE AND LIFE EXPERIENCES ARE VALUABLE! YOU ARE AN EXPERT!

(You don't have to be the expert to improve lives!)

☐ **ACTION STEP #2**

What are you an expert at? How can you improve lives? Write your answers:

IS YOUR BRAIN A LITTLE CLEANER NOW?

It's true, I am trying to brainwash you. I hope to get rid of the garbage in your brain telling you you aren't good enough or smart enough and fill the space with true facts about you!

Now that you're clear on how valuable your knowledge/product/service is...

Offer some of your value FOR FREE.

Many will say that giving your value away for free shows weakness and desperation. I completely disagree and have tons of proof that freely sharing what you know or what you have to offer shows confidence and connects you with the right people - people who will hire you or buy from you in the future.

When I began writing my first book in 2015, I was nervous about publishing my work on LinkedIn. I thought I was giving too much of my hard work away for free. THANK GOD I pushed through that fear! If I hadn't taken my audience along on my book writing journey, I would have missed out on making many great connections on LinkedIn! The universe repaid me for sharing my knowledge and hard work FOR FREE: I built a large group of followers on LinkedIn, many of which were moms who went to my website and joined my email list, and I made a valuable connection that landed my book in Canada's largest book retail franchise!

(Get 50% off a copy of Money & The 39 Forever Mom with the code FEMPRENEUR at yycfempreneur.com/goodreads.)

As I gained confidence in what I had to offer, I decided to make a video sharing my personal stories - the reasons **WHY** I was writing a book about money for moms. That video, full of *Ummm*'s, *Ahhhh*'s and *Soooo-Ya*'s, was the beginning of me showing my ideal clients, (moms) that I care about them and I can relate to them.

Your level of CARE equals your level of COURAGE!

This is especially true when making your first video and sharing it on social media!

One of the first action steps my coach assigned me, two weeks before I actually began writing material that later became my book, was to create an online survey. I had zero tech experience at this point in my life. I had not been introduced to surveymonkey.com nor did I have a website, a Facebook page or Instagram for my business. All I had was a LinkedIn profile which I had created around the time I hired my business coach.

My coach: *"Your assignment is to create a survey asking moms 39 and over what they want to achieve financially and what they feel is holding them back. Then you need to put your survey online."*
Me: *"Ok. How do I make an online survey?"*
My coach: *"You'll figure it out."*

I got to work building my survey in Pages on my Mac computer. Before trying to figure out how to put my survey online, I wanted to make sure it made sense and didn't have any errors, so I emailed the survey PDF to a few of my clients, my mom and my aunt. They gave me great ideas for additional questions and improved the wording. Although the feedback they gave me was very helpful, this is one of the, as my son would say, _cringiest_ memories of my business journey because my mom, my aunt and my clients were not my Dream Team. They didn't understand writing a book or building a business or using social media to attract my ideal clients. This memory made me realize I was **SO LONELY** back then! When I think of the incredible team of Fempreneurs I have right now, including you reading this, I am hugely grateful. I don't know where I'd be without all of you like-minded ladies!!

Before we continue, I want to remind you of the importance of staying connected to your team.

Have you met with your partner this week?

Do you have your next three partner meetings scheduled?

If you're serious about making positive change in your life, you will make time for your Fempreneur teammate(s)!

The Ultimate Conversation Opener

In the next chapter you're going to create a survey. That survey will have the power to open up many conversations with the right people because the best way to open a conversation is by asking a great question.

Get this: marketing magic will happen just from you asking your ideal clients to complete your survey, even though most of them won't actually complete it!

It's true - they don't need to actually complete the survey to begin to like and trust you!

Once my survey for "39 Forever Moms" was on surveymonkey.com, I ordered business cards online with the survey link on them. I began passing the cards out to all the 39+ moms I knew and a few I met at my local grocery store. I said I was writing a book for moms about money and I would like to know their opinion on which financial concepts more women need to understand. Here's what happened:

VERY FEW WOMEN TOOK MY SURVEY.

I felt disappointed and a bit rejected.

My business coach warned me this would happen and explained that the purpose of the survey was NOT to get 100 responses. It was to:

1. Position myself as *AN EXPERT* in my field

2. *BUILD TRUST* with my ideal clients by showing them I care

3. Get better at communicating with my ideal clients *IN THEIR LANGUAGE*

Guess what? It worked.

As the months passed and I began writing my book, I found myself using phrases from my survey over and over. I felt more professional. I was OWNING MY PURPOSE by declaring it over and over and effectively communicating that I had value to offer moms who were struggling financially. The simple exercise of writing a survey helped me feel more confident, like a true expert in my field.

What about the women who said they would take my survey and never did?

Here's what: Many of them told me to my face that they admired me for taking the time to ask women what they needed help with in a survey. I was now front of mind as the go-to person who cares deeply about helping women feel more financially secure.

"May I have your opinion on…?" Is a powerful way to open a conversation.

Once you've started the conversation, you need to HOOK them by providing a way for them to TAKE ACTION.

HOOK = "Here's how you can take action!"

The type of hook I use with a survey is a thank you gift. The thank you gift I offered with my 39 Forever Mom survey was the option to receive a draft chapter of my upcoming book in their inbox every couple of weeks. If they felt that was valuable to them, they could TAKE ACTION by joining my email list.

Here are some other hooks I've used in the past and will use again:

• A free 20 minute consultation

• $100 off coupon to be used for any of my services or courses

- A free ticket to a live or virtual event

- A free ebook (checklist or how-to guide) or online course

When your ideal clients trust you with their email address, it's A HUGE HONOUR. Give them something valuable in return.

As I got to work building my book, I hired a friend to build my website (before I began building websites for myself and others). He asked me if I had "Mailchimp". I had no clue what he was talking about. He explained that it was an email gathering system that also allowed me to build and send professional looking emails to my audience of subscribers. I said, "Yes please!".

Soon, my new website had a pop-up window that appeared in the first few seconds after someone arrived at my website. The pop-up used a word that I haven't used in years: newsletter. I've found much more creative ways to invite people to join my email list since then!

To grow my email audience, I began adding hooks to the articles I published on LinkedIn:

"You're invited to join my community for 39 Forever Moms! You'll receive tons of practical information to help you earn, save and invest better, right to your email inbox! ***Click here*** *to join!"*

This is also called a "Call To Action". It is important to have two or three of them in an article or blog post.

Adding hooks to my LinkedIn articles resulted in a growing Mailchimp email audience!

NOTE: If you don't have an email gathering system yet, now is a good time to go to Mailchimp.com and set up your free account!

The wording you use to invite people to take your survey and receive their free gift is your hook. When I was writing this book, here is the hook I used to invite women to take my survey:

"I'm writing a book to help tongue-tied, camera-shy women confidently share their message on social media. I discovered through building my own business, that my purpose is to share with women what I know about how to find your voice on social media. I'd like to know your opinion on what is holding most women back from confidently sharing their message on social media. To show my appreciation for your time, I have a free gift ($29.97 value) for you at the end of the survey!"

(The $29.97 free gift is 3 ebooks @ $9.99 each - 3 draft chapters from the upcoming book.)

When deciding on what to offer as your free gift, I recommend you choose something that will cost you zero money and very little to no time. As you saw on my list a few pages back (and as you noticed at fempreneurmarketing.com), my hooks are usually ebooks. If you sell products, this will be trickier, but not impossible. Your best bet if you sell products is to give a coupon to be used towards your products. An invitation to a live or virtual event works no matter what industry you're in, but it means you have to plan an event.

Not sure what to offer as a hook?
Do your research!

What are others in your industry offering in exchange for email addresses? If you are selling shoes, purses or anything fashion related, creating an ebook will be challenging. On the other hand, if you offer health or wellness products or services, you can definitely offer some of your knowledge for free in an ebook, online course or even a live event.

(If you are thinking about creating an ebook or a video of you sharing helpful information, you are going to LOVE the next two chapters!)

Here are some examples of topics for ebooks, videos and live and virtual courses. I hope these examples will inspire new ideas for ways you can share your knowledge and serve your people!

MY TOP 3 DAILY SUPPLEMENTS
THE RESEARCH BEHIND MY GO-TO HEALTH AND WELLNESS PRODUCTS

5 THINGS I WISH I'D KNOWN IN HIGH SCHOOL
HOW I OVERCAME SELF-DOUBT AND BECAME A BETTER HUMAN

HOW TO TAKE A GREAT SELFIE
MY FIVE SELFIE SUCCESS SECRETS

INSTAGRAM STORIES BASICS
THE HOW-TO GUIDE FOR INSTAGRAM NEWBIES

MY ON-THE-GO WORKOUT ROUTINE
PERFECT FOR HOTEL ROOMS, YOUR AUNT'S BASEMENT + JUST ABOUT ANYWHERE!

5 MUST-HAVE WARDROBE ITEMS
HOW TO STAY IN-STYLE + IN YOUR BUDGET

HOW TO WRITE A GREAT SPEECH
IN FIVE SIMPLE STEPS

Creating a free ebook or educational video is a great way to help your clients get immediate results and experience your value first hand. This keeps them answering "Yes!" to those two key questions:

Can she help me? - *YES!*
Does she care about me? - *YES!*

NOTE: You will learn more about creating ebooks and other knowledge products in the "Create" chapter. Stay tuned!

☐ ACTION STEP #3

Work with your partner to brainstorm what you can offer for free in your hook and write your ideas below:

☐ ACTION STEP #4

Write your hook using the HOOK FORMULA:

1. Describe their **AMBITION** ("their" being the people you want to serve) - *"I'm writing a book to help tongue-tied, camera-shy women confidently share their message on social media."*

2. Short personal story explaining **WHY** you care - *"I discovered through building my own business that my purpose is to share with women what I know about how to find your voice on social media."*

3. **ASK** for their opinion - *"I'd like to know your opinion on what is holding most women back from confidently sharing their message on social media."*

4. Offer **VALUE**: FREE GIFT(S) - <u>always state the value $$$</u> - *"To show my appreciation for your time, I have a free gift - $29.97 value - for you at the end of the survey!"*

Congratulations on writing your first hook!

You now have the paragraph you will post on social media when you invite people to take your survey in the next chapter!

NOTE: Never Discount Ten Email Subscribers.

Meet Sally. Two weeks ago, Sally posted her new free ebook on social media with what she thought was a great hook. Sally now has only ten new email subscribers. She's feeling a little bummed.

Sally feels bummed because she is discounting her ten email subscribers.

Have you ever felt like Sally, frustrated and a little pouty because you have "only ten" people interested in your amazing new offer, especially when it is FREE?

Ask yourself these two questions the next time you aren't getting the response you hoped for when you put yourself out there:

1. If you continue to offer value and show you care in the emails you send those ten ladies, ten ladies who trust you enough to give you their email address, do you think they will tell their friends about you?

2. DO YOU THINK THAT EACH OF THOSE TEN EMAIL SUBSCRIBERS HAS TEN FRIENDS?

Never discount ten email subscribers.

Starting a conversation with ten people who want to learn from you and see you as an expert is a HUGE WIN! The hardest part of a conversation is starting it.

Reminder: marketing is just conversation!

The hardest part of learning how to start meaningful conversations online is learning how to trust yourself. As you believe in yourself and the value you have to offer more and more, you will begin to confidently share your message on social media and serve more and more of the people you want to serve.

Meet my friend Hanna Bracken…

As a child, I always wanted to fit in, be that in my own family, my birth country (Finland) and the country that raised me: Canada.

I was often told I was too sensitive. Growing up in a small town in British Columbia, I was bullied at school for being different, an immigrant, so I learned to put on a brave face.

I desperately wanted to fit in and find a place to belong. The place I always felt I fit the best and could be myself was with my animals. When I was with my animals, I was more creative and intuitive.

People saw me as a serious girl, but really, I wore the "Mask of Fine". Inside, I was lost, confused, depressed - anything but "fine". I learned to lose myself in the emotions of others around me in order to keep the peace. I didn't know where I began or ended. I felt everyone's emotions and was internally overloaded all the time. My animals were my peaceful escape.

Thanks to my animals, I eventually learned that I do fit in with the most important person: MYSELF! Animals have taught me that true courage and strength lies in one's ability to be vulnerable, to admit when they're <u>not fine.</u>

Letting go of my "brave face" has allowed me to revisit and comprehend the range of emotions I experienced in my life: losing my animal companions, wanting to end my life after an assault, surviving two emergency surgeries and forgiving my father after his ten year absence from my life.

Looking back on my childhood, everything shaped and prepared me to become the woman I am today. I am now happy to be called either "too sensitive" or, "an empath".

As I became more confident in who I am, I began exploring the idea of working with animals as a career. I wanted to help people understand their animals better.

My belief in the healing power of animals led me to training with the Gurney Institute of Animal Communication in California. The program took me three and a half years to complete.

The journey to making a career from my passion was challenging. During my studies, my father-in-law was diagnosed with four different types of cancer before he passed away, all the while my father was battling Alzheimers.

So many times, I thought, "I should put my training on the back burner for now. I should focus on my family. I'll resume my training when my life is less hectic." Whenever this thought came into my head, thankfully, my purpose won. Plus, I knew my father and father-in-law would want me to keep moving forward in building my career. (Nothing worth having comes easy.)

The day my dad passed away, I was in California completing the final module of my Animal Communication studies. There are no words for that moment, other than I am immensely grateful for the support of my friends and the animals I was working with.

What I realized after my dad passed away is what I want you to take away from this story:

NO MATTER WHAT LIFE THROWS AT YOU, YOUR PASSION WILL DRIVE YOU TO KEEP GOING AND STAND UP FOR YOURSELF THE WAY YOU DO FOR OTHERS.

Soon after becoming a Certified Animal Communicator, I knew I needed to launch a website and share my passion to help people and their animals. I got to work on building my website and setting up my social media accounts. I started blogging and writing a monthly newsletter. My clientele began to grow. I continued volunteering with the Gurney Institute as a mentor to new students of their Animal Communication program.

Two years into my business, I heard of the YYC Fempreneur Marketing School. Shortly after I registered, Lyndsie was passing through Golden BC, where I live, and we met for coffee. We each shared stories about what led us to discovering our purpose and three hours later, we said goodbye. That day was the beginning of a new friendship with not only Lyndsie but with my soon-to-be Fempreneur Marketing School classmates.

One of the biggest changes I made in my marketing since completing Lyndsie's program is the way I open conversations with my audience on social media and in my blog and newsletter. I now share more stories about my past, both the traumatic stories and the heart warming stories. I am more comfortable with sharing photos and videos of myself because I see the value in the human connection that photos and videos create with my audience online.

When things get tough or I feel overwhelmed, I take a breath and think back of what I have walked through in my life and where I have come from. I stop and take another breath and keep going knowing I have found my passion and I know my purpose. I know I am meant to serve and help others.

During 2019, I found my voice on social media and began confidently sharing my message:

I am here to help people navigate through one of life's most difficult challenges: losing an animal.

When life challenges you and you feel like quitting, you are being tested and strengthened. You are being taught how to dig even deeper into believing in yourself and your purpose. Once you've seen clearly what you are made of, building a website and sharing your message on social media is easy in comparison!

Hanna Bracken
www.hannabracken.com
f @ @hanna_bracken

"By showing up for yourself, you are showing up for those you serve."

-Hanna Bracken

DREAM TEAM REMINDER

Conversations between women are often consumed with topics like celebrities and other meaningless gossip. Conversations between women can also be consumed with negativity, if we aren't mindful of our intention for the conversation. We all have that friend we can go to with our problems or when we just need a laugh, which all women need, but let's look at another type of conversation right now:

Be Intentional.

While you are building your Dream Team, be intentional during coffee or walk dates with women you don't know well. I'm not saying you should turn every coffee or walk into a business meeting, but I encourage you to discuss goals, dreams and plans to achieve big things. Without an intention to dig deep by asking bold, meaningful questions, the conversation can quickly become about other people and things that, in the long run, will have zero effect on our lives.

If you are getting to know a new woman, (and you are secretly interviewing her for your Dream Team), notice if she is comfortable sharing what she's excited about or what she hopes to achieve over the next few months. Notice (don't judge) how she talks about herself and others and how she responds when you share with her what you're working on. Is she comfortable with deep, meaningful conversation? It may take a few conversations to get her to open up and be real with you, so don't expect to be able to decide if she's "Dream Team Material" after the first encounter!

However, if it's clear she doesn't want to talk about goals and dreams, she probably isn't a good fit for your Dream Team right now. Tell her you're here for her and move on, but keep in touch with her, because timing is everything.

NOTE: If you sell products or services, never allow your mind to focus on what you can gain from her. Stay connected to your intention to learn about her, be inspired by her and to be real with her.

As Hanna just shared in her story, the first time I met her was when I was passing through Golden BC. During our first ever coffee meeting, I shared lots of personal information with her, my goals and challenges, and asked her to do the same. We both opened ourselves up to a new friendship and came away with a friend and teammate!

Keep building your dream team one authentic, inspiring woman at a time!

☐ ACTION STEP #5

Look at your *SMASH LIST* in your notebook or on page 50 of this book. Choose a goal from the list to add to your goal board and write it in the week 2 box. Add a deadline date to your goal.

If you're having trouble adding a deadline date to your goal, it's because it's a BIG GOAL that will require many steps to achieve. These steps are micro goals. Ask you partner to help you break your BIG GOAL into smaller steps, each with a deadline date and a checkbox.

For example, when I decided to write my first book, I created a goal board that stated my goals and a deadline for each goal. The deadline is not an actual "dead" line, meaning you won't die if you don't achieve that goal by the date you aimed to! Don't be afraid to set a date because you don't like missing deadlines. Be brave, set your intention, do the work and if you need to push the deadline back by a few days or weeks, it's OK.

Here's the big goal I set that I ended up achieving six weeks later than my original deadline:

"Complete my book by July 1st."

This is when I learned about breaking big goals down into micro goals, because "Write a Book" is a HUGE GOAL. Underneath that goal there should be a list of micro goals, each with a deadline.

Here are some examples of goals you may want to achieve and how you can break them down into micro goals:

BIG GOAL EXAMPLE: "Start my podcast"

☐ Announce podcast launch date (on social media and to my email subscribers) on _____, 20XX (two weeks before launch date)

☐ Record three podcast episodes by _____, 20XX

☐ Edit all three episodes by _____, 20XX

☐ Set up podcast on Squarespace.com and post a teaser episode to make sure it works on Google, Apple and Spotify by _____, 20XX

☐ Go live on Facebook on podcast launch day with a friend (interview style) to share the story behind why you started a podcast and who it is for. _____, 20XX

BIG GOAL EXAMPLE: "Find the answer to X"

☐ Call some people and have three interviews scheduled by _____, 20XX

☐ Complete two hours of online research on _____, 20XX

☐ Listen to three podcast episodes on this topic by _____, 20XX

BIG GOAL EXAMPLE: "Publish a new blog post every 2 weeks"

☐ Schedule three consecutive hours to write each week starting on _____, 20XX

☐ Find a writing accountability partner who will read and edit your work (and you will do the same for her) by _____, 20XX

☐ Publish your first blog post on _____, 20XX

BIG GOAL EXAMPLE: "Launch my online course"

These are the steps I took to create my "Own Your Purpose" online course.

<u>Note:</u> *I invited ten women to take the live course for free on Zoom, I recorded it, then I used the recordings as the paid online course.*

☐ Choose the three topics to cover in the course (one per session) by _____, 20XX

☐ Create an image at canva.com with the course and dollar value by _____, 20XX

☐ Record a video explaining why you built this course, the problem solves and what it's worth (dollar value $$$) and that there are only 10 spots by _____, 20XX

☐ Start a Facebook group chat with 20 women who need this free course. Post the video in the group chat and send them to a sign up link by _____, 20XX

☐ Build the community: A week before Session One, in the Facebook group chat, ask the ladies to share their WHY story in a video by _____, 20XX

☐ Build Session One (a day or two before the first live training session) _____, 20XX (repeat for Session Two and Three)

☐ Edit all three videos by _____, 20XX

☐ Create a profile at moonclerk.com, add the "Digital Delivery" package and upload course by _____, 20XX

☐ Create and test links to the course on your website and email a special limited time offer - 30% off - to email subscribers on _____, 20XX

Now you're ready to write a BIG GOAL with macro goals underneath on your goal board!

Tell me how you're doing!

I'd love to know what you've achieved so far and what your goals are! Please share a photo of your goal board on Instagram or Facebook and tag **@yycfempreneurs**, or message it to me! I want to cheer you on!

☐ ACTION STEP #6

Schedule grad night! With your team, plan a night to celebrate your completion of Fempreneur Marketing School! The final chapter, "Let's Party", will help you make it an exciting and memorable night!

SHOW OFF YOUR SUCCESS!

Once you've completed all the action steps from this week and met with your partner, print and add the CONVERSATION BADGE to your goal board! Find it at fempreneurmarketing.com/week2.

2.
CONVERSATION
Chapter Summary

- People assign value to the products/services you offer by asking themselves, *"Can she help me solve my problem?"* and, *"Do I like her?"*

- You don't have to be THE expert. You are AN EXPERT and your knowledge combined with your unique life experiences are VALUABLE!

- Never forget the importance of staying connected to your team. Make it a priority to meet with your partner each week.

- Sharing some of your value for free shows confidence and connects you with the right people, people who will hire you or buy from you in the future.

- The purpose of creating a survey is NOT to get 100 responses. It is to:
    1. Position you as *AN EXPERT* in your field.
    2. *BUILD TRUST.*
    3. Improve your ability to communicate with your ideal clients *IN THEIR LANGUAGE.*

- Never discount ten email subscribers. (Do you think they each have ten friends?)

- Entice your ideal clients to take your survey with a **HOOK**: a valuable thank you gift!

- If you want to **HOOK** people with an ebook or a video of you sharing helpful information, you are going to LOVE the next two chapters!

- When life challenges you and you feel like quitting, you are being tested and strengthened.

- *"By showing up for yourself, you are showing up for those you serve."* -Hanna Bracken

For the first four years in my finance career, I worked with anyone who had a heartbeat and a bank account. I didn't know who my ideal client was, nor did I like the idea of being "niche". I didn't want to say no to potential business, no matter how wrong the client was for me.

As time went on, my group of clients became predominantly moms. This wasn't my intention and I didn't even realize it until my business coach asked me to paint a picture of my ideal client. He asked me to think of my favourite clients and describe them. It turned out, they were all women, and mostly moms.

Why do you think I had a higher success rate with women, especially moms?

Because I am a mom.

"The riches are in the niches."
~ Pat Flynn

During client meetings and on social media, I shared my stories of my small town upbringing, becoming a hairdresser and a single working mom. The people who could relate to me the most were the ones I built relationships with the fastest.

If you're not sharing stories about your life on social media as a way to connect with the people you want to serve, you're missing out on something Pat Flynn calls *Your Unfair Advantage* in his awesome book, Will It Fly.

As I gained confidence in my abilities and tailored my marketing to talk specifically to moms, it became easier to write my blog posts and send emails to my audience. I knew who I was talking to. When someone unsubscribed from my audience, I was OK with that. It meant they couldn't relate to what I was saying.

Serving the wrong people for a while is an important part of gaining confidence and figuring out who you actually want to serve, but it's time to step into your purpose to serve a specific group of people!

Sure, you are a talented, driven woman who can help all sorts of people with all sorts of problems, but it's really difficult to market to a wide range of people with a wide range of problems.

Have you ever been at a restaurant where the menu had waaaaaay too many options?

You want a short, specific description of who you serve and a short, specific list of the ways you serve them.

Whether you're asking people to take a survey or you're having a sale at your Etsy store, this must be at the root of your message on social media:

"My core desire is to serve you."

Who is the "YOU" in that statement?

☐ ACTION STEP #1

Describe the person you feel called to serve in the space below. Include personality traits, values, possibly age and gender, and a list of the problems he/she is facing that you can help with:

Immediately after high school, I learned that if I wanted to be successful at anything, I had to actually care about helping others. My dad wanted me to get out of my small hometown and experience city life, so he arranged for me to live with my step-sister in Vancouver. She promptly introduced me to new books and perspectives and people. I pictured myself as a business owner. I caught a glimpse of "Adult Lyndsie" who could succeed at business stuff and share her knowledge with others, developing products and services to improve lives.

My step-sister was in Amway, which was her key source of self-development and entrepreneurial inspiration. At age 18, I joined Amway, and half-heartedly tried to build that business for the next four years. The few events I attended and the people I met through Amway changed my life for the better by teaching me to go out into the world with a servant mentality, work hard, listen intently, smile lots and take risks. Getting to know people who were actively pursuing the life they want - a life they designed - inspired me and prepared me for my future as a business owner.

These are the foundational concepts I learned from Amway:

1. Read How To Win Friends & Influence People by Dale Carnegie to become more service-minded. The most important lesson I gained from this book was how to *Be Genuinely Interested in Others*. *(There's a great updated version of this book, which was originally written in 1936 - find it at: fempreneurmarketing.com/goodreads.)*

2. Gain an understanding of how residual income works and explore ways you can build a few residual income streams to fuel your purpose and lifestyle. **It takes profit to sustain a purpose.**

3. If you come from a school or family that taught you very little about money, business and investing, find mentors who are building the success they desire.

The key marketing lesson I learned in Dale Carnegie's famous book, How To Win Friends and Influence People, is:

People are selfish.

Looking out for number one is in our DNA - a survival instinct. This fact is the reason Dale Carnegie's book set me up for not only marketing success, but also taught me how to be a good servant:

I learned at age 18 to talk to people about their #1 priority: THEMSELVES!

Being selfish isn't a bad thing. It's a result of thousands of years of trying to stay alive without houses, cars, furnaces and medicine. However, our selfishness does pose a challenge to people like you and I who need to effectively communicate our message of, *"I'm here to serve you"*: we need to become less selfish!

Every person has a problem they want solved, a problem they will pay someone to take away. That's what they think about most. Start a conversation with them about it.

Like we talked about in the last chapter, a survey is one of the best ways to start conversations with the people you want to serve by asking them to:

1.   DESCRIBE THEIR IDEAL OUTCOME. If their specific problem was solved, what would that look like?

2. SHARE WHAT'S HOLDING THEM BACK. Ask them what they need from an expert like you. Is it education? Is it a community of people dealing with the same struggle? Is it a service or product?

Find out specifically what roadblocks they need help smashing through and give them options for how they would want to move forward, in an ideal world.

When you invite people to take your survey, or launch any sort of product or service, there's a good chance you will be faced with...

Judgement & Crickets.

Many times, I built things no one wanted and had to push through the feeling that I had missed the mark. The great news is, these were the moments when I learned the most valuable lessons, which I am so excited to share with you in this book!

Here's what I tell myself when I feel judged or rejected:

"I would rather earn money doing something I love ON MY TERMS rather than working at a job or for a company that doesn't get me excited to jump out of bed in the morning."

Here's what I ask myself when I'm getting ready to launch or post something big and bold, before I know whether or not it will be well received:

"What's the worst that can happen?"

What if people don't welcome your offer to serve them with open arms? What if someone comments negatively below one of your posts? What if your mom or aunt or sister texts you and asks, *"Are you okay?"* after seeing something you just posted on Facebook? What if you plan a workshop and the only two people who register are your best friends?

Literally every single one of those things has happened to me and some worse things.

Here's what I suggest you do to prepare yourself for the inevitable (judgement and crickets):

Surround yourself with like-minded women.

Judgement will always sting a little. The best way to minimize the sting is to get around women who are taking similar risks so you can learn and grow together.

Judgement from others is the world telling you to <u>KEEP GOING.</u>

(The person who just posted a negative comment heard your message loud and clear. This is a <u>good</u> thing!)

Rejection doesn't mean NO, it means, <u>"Not right now"</u> or, <u>"Not like that"</u>.

Rejection is actually just crickets, and there are lessons in the crickets - extremely valuable lessons!!

Look for the lessons in the crickets.

If you are offering something big like a new product, service or event, hearing crickets means you need to repackage it and try again in a few months.

If you are posting something you feel is big and bold on social media and you are looking for conversations to come from it, the crickets mean you need to try saying it a different way at a later time.

Although crickets are better than a full-blown "No!", it can still be frustrating. This is when you need your team.

I'd like to introduce you to a member of my team, Stacey Watts…

Not long ago, I was ready to quit my business. I was a solo-preneur feeling overwhelmed and alone. I was passionate about helping business owners build their brand on social media, but I was quickly losing my gusto. I felt burned out, like something had to give. I couldn't figure out how to serve both my clients and my family. I began to doubt myself and I just wanted to run away, to end the one thing I thought was the problem: my business.

I came across the YYC Fempreneurs on social media and realized the woman running it was my old hairdresser, Lyndsie Barrie, who I hadn't seen in eight years. We ran into each other at one event, then another. Both times I saw her, she was with a gang of female business owners and they looked like they were having a great time learning together and supporting one another. That's when I realized the answer to my problem:

"I need a supportive team of business women who understand me!"

I took Lyndsie's free six week marketing school and met the most amazing women. Lyndsie and I met for coffee to discuss how I could shift the way I serve my clients. I shared with her the story of one of Canada's original "mompreneurs", my grandma, Betty.

My grandma said something to me right after I left the corporate world to start my own marketing and communications business, something that spurred me on whenever I felt overwhelmed in my business…

Before I tell you what she said to me, you need to understand the person that is my grandma.

My grandma opened up her own business in her garage in 1959 in my hometown, Niverville Manitoba. The business was our town's Post Office. She was one of the first female Postmasters in Canada. My grandma was also a mom at the time.

Around the time she became Niverville's Postmaster, she also took on a volunteer position for the local newspaper, writing interesting stories each week. For 31 years, my grandma continued to compile the news and tell the Niverville story.

My grandma was a leader in both 4H and the Explorers and Canada Girls in Training (CGIT). She also served on the executive of the Niverville Chamber of Commerce, was secretary treasurer of the Niverville Community Club and planned our curling club's bonspiels for 20 years.

When it came to her household duties, grandma got up every morning and baked bread or made waffles on the cast iron waffle maker before starting her day's work as Postmaster. She also prepared a lunch for my grandfather who worked an hour from home. When her children came home from school for lunch every day, they were greeted by their mom and a home-cooked meal.

This lifestyle was rare in the 60's. Women didn't own businesses, especially not married women. My grandparents were a very progressive couple, sharing the "pink and blue jobs". There was no day care, because there were so few working moms.

When us grandchildren came along, my grandma would cook a huge, delicious meal and have us over for dinner every Sunday.

It wasn't until I became a mom that I reflected on the similarities between the life my grandma led and the life her daughter, my mom, led. My mom was one of the first female school bus drivers in Niverville, Manitoba. She, like my grandma, worked from home, because the bus sat in our driveway. She also coached my baseball team for a few seasons and volunteered in other areas of our community.

I think it is so valuable to see your parent, whether a mom or dad, work from home, just like kids who grow up on farms see the day to day actions that result in paying the bills. Since my grandpa worked an hour away, my grandma was the one who showed her kids what "work", not just housework, actually looked like.

Because of the legacy my grandma left and the values she instilled in me, it is hugely important to me that my kids see me as a "working mom". I am grateful that they actually get to see what I do to bring money into our household, money that helps pay for their vacations and food and sports, all the things most kids take for granted.

What my grandma said to me when I left the corporate world,

which seems harsh to read in text, but I felt so much love coming from her when she said it, was this:

"Oh good! You get to be a real mom now!"

She was excited for me and proud that I was following in her footsteps. She wanted what was best for my two young sons, my husband and me. It was clear when she said, "Oh good! You get to be a real mom now!" she believed what was best for me was to quit my job downtown Calgary so I could finish my degree in Media and Communications, start my own business, work from home and serve my family and community.

The reason my grandma's words still spur me on is I believe the opportunity to serve both my family and my community is a gift that women had to fight hard for. Women weren't respected as business owners and leaders for centuries. Plus, I know I have what it takes to serve my community and be a great mom because my mom and grandma were great examples when I was growing up.

In the moments when I feel I am not enough or I'm not doing a good enough job at covering all the bases, I give myself more grace than I used to. I channel my inner Grandma Betty, strive for progress over perfection and I take better care of myself now.

A huge part of taking care of myself is making time to get around other mompreneurs, to share and learn with them. Often, just hearing that she understands the challenges I'm facing because she's facing them too makes me feel like a huge weight has been lifted off my shoulders!

If you think it will be too hard to run your own business from home, or if you have your own business and you want to quit, do what I did:

PIVOT. DON'T QUIT.

Shift your mindset. The best way to do this is to get around other women who have similar dreams and values, women who are going for it and are willing to share what's working and not working for them.

If you know you need to make some changes to avoid burning out, here's what I suggest you do...

Stacey Watts
www.upvirtualcommunications.com
f @ @upvirtualcommunications

"Get around more women in business who are striving to be better, do more and improve the lives of others."
- Stacey Watts

How do we Fempreneurs toughen up in those painful moments when all we can hear is crickets and/or negative comments?

Here's what I hear over and over when I ask women why they won't quit when the going gets tough:

- Doing uncomfortable things is often linked to positive results.

- I want to work with the right people.

- I am ready to open myself up to discovering what's next in my life.

- I know taking risks is essential to getting my own business off the ground so I can quit my unfulfilling job.

- I'm determined to figure out what effective marketing is and how to do it.

- I'm ready to make my ideas come to life.

If you'd like to hear more women share their reasons for staying strong, go to fempreneurmarketing.com/podcast and listen to a few episodes!

Fear kills more dreams than failure ever will.

Don't be afraid of messing up or what others might think of your big, bold attempts to serve others. Surround yourself with others like you and the big, bold things you are doing won't seem as scary!

Picture the people you are meant to serve.

That's who you will fail if you quit.

☐ ACTION STEP #2

Why won't you quit when the going gets tough? Write your answers below and look back on this list whenever you need help telling fear: "Beat it!"

☐ ACTION STEP #3

Flip back in this chapter to Action Step #1. Take a picture of the description you wrote for the person you feel called to serve. Send the photo in a message to your partner and share it in your group chat, too. Get your team's help with clarifying your niche by asking them, *"What else do I need to know about my ideal client so I can become more niche?"* You can also ask them, *"Is it clear who I am trying to serve?"*

☐ ACTION STEP #4

Brainstorm a list of 5-7 multiple choice survey questions in your notebook or on the next page. As you write, keep reminding yourself that the goal of the survey is to understand the problem your ideal client is facing and to get better at communicating in THEIR LANGUAGE.

Multiple choice survey question **EXAMPLES:**

1. Describe 3-5 different ideal outcomes and ask them pick their favourite.

2. Write 3-5 specific roadblocks you can help them smash through and ask them to pick the one that is most important to them.

3. List 3-5 methods of gaining information, such as live events, ebooks, video courses, audio recordings and paperback books, and ask them to choose their go-to method of learning.

Use the space provided to brainstorm your questions:

Head to fempreneurmarketing.com/week3 to see survey examples and a video on how to create a great survey. MAKE SURE TO WATCH THE VIDEO, but in case you miss me saying this in the video, here is what your survey needs to have:

- **5-6 multiple choice questions**

- **Provide an "other" option for all multiple choice questions**

- **1-2 comment questions (respondents will answer in their own words)**

- **No more than 7 questions total**

Keep in mind this is your first draft survey - *it is not the final cut!* Don't allow yourself to be frozen in perfectionism! Keep moving forward! Ask for help if you need it! And if you feel someone on your team is stuck, offer to help her! Building a survey is a tough but necessary step in fulfilling your purpose.

☐ ACTION STEP #5

Put your survey online using the instructions at fempreneurmarketing.com/week3.

☐ ACTION STEP #6

Add your HOOK from last week as your intro paragraph and share your survey link in your team's group chat.

☐ ACTION STEP #7

Take every one of your teammates' surveys and provide honest, helpful feedback in the comment box at the end of their surveys. Do this before your week four group session. The surveys need to be ready for the public by the end of week 4.

Reminder: survey creation steps are described in detail with updated technology instructions at <u>fempreneurmarketing.com/week3</u>.

When you are giving feedback to your teammates, try to answer both of these questions clearly and with love:

1.   Did she clearly communicate who should take the survey in the intro paragraph?

2.   Did she position herself as an expert in her field and as someone who cares about serving others?

If you have suggestions to improve her survey, share them with her. When giving feedback, it is just as important to encourage as it is to constructively criticize. Here are ways to accomplish this when giving feedback:

1.   List the things you liked first. If there was not one thing you actually liked, choose something that was the closest to good and start with that.

2. Whenever possible, turn your suggestion into a question. For example, *"What do you think of wording it this way instead…?"*

☐ ACTION STEP #8

Update your goal board! Check off the big goals and micro goals you have accomplished and add a new goal or two. Something I like to do is write things I've accomplished on my goal board and immediately check them off! Have fun with your goal board and when you look at it, smile and tell yourself you have done FANTASTIC WORK!

Your goal board should look something like this by the end of week 3:

My Goals

SHOW OFF YOUR SUCCESS!

Once you've completed all the action steps from this week and met with your partner, print and add the SERVICE BADGE to your goal board! Find it at <u>fempreneurmarketing.com/week3</u>.

3.
SERVICE
Chapter Summary

- The people who can relate to you the most are the ones you will build relationships with the fastest.

- Nothing says "I am an expert" like being <u>NICHE.</u>

- Talk to people about their #1 priority: <u>THEMSELVES!</u>

- Judgement from others is the world telling you to <u>KEEP GOING.</u> (The person who just posted a negative comment heard your message loud and clear. This is a <u>good</u> thing!)

- Rejection doesn't mean NO, it means, *"Not right now"* or *"Not like that"*. Therefore, it is not rejection. It's crickets.

- Look for the lessons in the crickets.

- *"Get around more women in business who are striving to be better, do more and improve the lives of others."* - Stacey Watts

- Fear kills more dreams than failure ever will.

- Understand the problem your ideal client is facing and get better at communicating in THEIR LANGUAGE by creating a survey.

- When giving feedback, list the things you liked first and try turning your suggestions in to questions, like, *"Do you think this sounds better ..."*.

- *Have fun with your goal board and when you look at it, smile and tell yourself you have done FANTASTIC WORK!*

Cynthia, a retired RCMP member, joined Fempreneur Marketing School without a business or even a desire to start a business. She was writing a book about PTSD (post-traumatic stress disorder) and had a big speaking engagement coming up. Her vocal coach Emma Rushton had recently graduated from Fempreneur Marketing School and recommended the program to Cynthia. I am so grateful that Emma did that because getting to know Cynthia and watching her find her voice as a speaker, author and mental health advocate has been a huge pleasure.

Meet Cynthia…

As adults, we are all impacted by events that occurred during our childhood years. We watch, we listen, and we learn. Some messaging is clear and direct: don't take things that don't belong to you. Some messages are more subtle: if we share our toys, everyone can get along. Then, there are those messages that are unintended consequences of well-meaning behaviour. This a story about the unintended consequences of a parenting decision. A decision that my parents believed would make me a better person.

"Maybe this time he won't find me," I said to my nine-year-old self, knowing darn well that wouldn't be the case. I positioned the coats in front of me, after quietly closing the closet door. The scent of cigarette smoke and perfume hung in the air as I waited for the final count.

"Ready or not, here I come!" my brother shouted. I stood quietly, but he came right for me, as he always did... "No fair!" I yelled for the hundredth time.

I'm sure just about every one of you has played Hide-N-Go Seek at some point in your life. I loved playing with the neighbourhood kids, but with my brother, not so much. When I played with the kids on my street, I got to home base half the time. When I played with my brother, I never won. It was so frustrating. He was two years older than me, so he did have that advantage, but that was never the issue. It was the other thing, the other advantage... he was blind.

My brother had a rare genetic disorder called Bardet-Biedl Syndrome, which took his eyesight by age nine. I imagine you are wondering how being blind could be an advantage. It was an advantage because with every bit of vision he lost, his sense of hearing increased. What he couldn't see, he could hear: my movement and my breathing. No matter where I hid, he found me.

That was, until I came up with a brilliant idea. I remember it so clearly. I realized that if I could hold my breath, I could win… finally! My brother was suspicious when I asked him to play because I rarely asked him. He was always the one initiating the play. We lived in a small, three bedroom bungalow. The "counter" would count in the family room and the "hider" would slip away. I still remember my brother counting, "…eight, nine, ten!" as I tiptoed behind the living-room curtain, waited until he was a little closer, and took a deep breath.

It worked. He walked right by me. I was thrilled… that was, until my lungs started burning. I needed to breathe! I told myself, just a little bit more, but couldn't hold on. I gasped like someone who had almost drowned, trying desperately to find more air.

That was it. Game over. My brother turned around, walked directly back to me and yelled, "It's not fair, she held her breath!" Knowing my parents would hear him, I yelled "It's not fair, he's blind and can hear me!"

I shuddered as I heard my parents footsteps heading in our direction. I knew this would be a battle I wouldn't win. The expressions on my parent's faces told me I was right. "What were you thinking? How could you do that to your brother? Don't you understand how hard life is for him?" The questions were fired at me like an automatic weapon, my heart breaking with each attack.

It was decided I needed to learn a lesson. Something harsh, something that would stay with me for a long time. I still remember the knot forming in my stomach when I heard my mother say, "Let's blindfold her. Let her see what it's like to be blind. One hour should do it." I turned to my father, hoping to see a sign he was in my court. There was none.

I stood in front of my mother as she told me to stand still, tying the itchy, smelly blindfold behind my head. As the light disappeared and I entered a dark, scary world, I had no idea the impact it would have on the rest of my life. I stood in the centre of the living room not wanting to move. In my mind, I could see the layout of the furniture and I could feel my parents watching me. Feeling defiant, I decided to stand right where I was until the hour was up. Of course, my mother ordered me to walk around, so I could really feel what it was like. As I moved toward the couch, I forgot about the coffee table sitting in front of it and banged my shin harshly on it's corner. The pain took my breath away. My tears, like my emotions, were absorbed by the scarf. Gone. Pushed aside, like they were never there in the first place.

My parents believed they were doing the right thing, teaching a young child a lesson in empathy. They meant well, but their methods were harsh. They also never considered, what my world may have been like having a disabled brother. They focused so much attention on him, that they missed a whole section of the story:

Me. My feelings.

They couldn't have been more wrong about things. I watched him struggle. I watched people make fun of him. I fought with kids who picked on him and I heard his frustrations when he couldn't see something. My heart broke for him all the time. It was a heavy burden for a child to carry.

That day, all I wanted, all I needed was a moment to feel like I really mattered. It wasn't what they said to me, but rather what they didn't say. They didn't say, it must be lonely and tough when your brother gets all the attention. They didn't say, it must be difficult when people stare at him. They didn't say, you must feel sad when you see him struggling. The unintended consequence of their parenting decision was what I learned that day: that my feelings didn't matter. I learned other people's feelings were more important than mine. At nine years old, I learned to tuck my feelings away, put them on a shelf, and never revisit them again. I continued to live my life that way until I couldn't.

Cynthia Hamilton Urquhart
www.cynthiahamiltonurquhart.com
f ⃝ @cynthiahamiltonurquhart

**"Learn how to find beauty in your brokenness."
- Cynthia Hamilton Urquhart**

Shortly after Cynthia retired from over 25 years serving as an RCMP member, she began experiencing the aftermath of years of trauma she put on a shelf, a shelf that finally couldn't hold any more weight. Part of her work with therapists was to write the stories that were stuck in her head, keeping her up at night.

The message she is sharing in her book, speeches and online through her "Mental Health Hub" is that *your feelings matter.* Moreover, your mental health matters. Cynthia wants to help people deal with the trauma they've experienced by sharing ways to find beauty in their brokenness.

I hope you'll connect with Cynthia, let her know you read her story in this book and learn more about her upcoming book!

Having Cynthia on my book project team was a huge gift. She reminded me over and over again as she proofread these pages to speak to women who don't think of themselves as businesswomen and feel intimidated by the word "marketing". I hope this book gets into the hands of many more women like Cynthia and inspires them to share their powerful stories, too.

Your personal stories are your "unfair advantage".

Like Cynthia's brother's impeccable hearing, you, too, have an *unfair advantage* due to your unique life circumstances. In fact, you have many unfair advantages, each one a story from your past. Although you may not consider yourself to be a business woman with competition, you have many unfair advantages over others who do the same thing you do.

For example, if Cynthia's website and LinkedIn profile said simply that she is a mental health advocate, speaker and author, do you think that she would stand out in a crowd of other women, with the same "resume", to someone looking to hire a speaker or purchase a book about mental health? There are other mental health advocates who are also speakers and authors, but do they all have blogs sharing stories like Cynthia's? No! Her stories are her unfair advantage.

If you aren't sharing the stuff that's happened to you to make you better at your career or simply a better person, you're missing out on unique ways that ONLY YOU can improve lives. Whether or not you own a business, your stories make you relatable to a specific group of people dealing with a specific problem.

NOTE: In this chapter, we are setting the foundation for offering paid products and services. If you feel you aren't ready for that yet, simply gather email addresses (Mailchimp.com) using the steps in this chapter. Whether or not you plan to have a business or "sell" anything, having a list of email addresses is vital to sharing your message with the right people.

If someone reads your post on social media (or watches your video) and feels curious about you, intrigued by your story and your personality, they will naturally look for the next steps. These "natural next steps" are ways people can get to know you better or schedule a meeting with or buy from you.

Here are the most common "Natural Next Steps" (ways to take action) in no particular order:

One of the natural next steps is a social follow or like, but we aren't going to talk about how to increase social media followers in this chapter. Let's assume everyone who sees you share your story on social media is already following you.

Here's why are we not focusing on increasing your social media followers in this chapter:

There is no guarantee your social media followers will see your posts.

You want to be able to have conversations via <u>email</u> with your audience.

You want more email addresses so that when you are ready to monetize your talents, you have a list of people who like and trust you. Again, your social media followers will not see everything you post on your Facebook page or Instagram profile.

This chapter will help you prepare to use <u>your stories</u> as a way to start real conversations and convert social media followers into email subscribers.

If you're brand new to sharing stories or posting anything on social media, you're about to learn how to share your valuable message with a clear purpose behind each and every post.

If you've been posting for a while on your social media channel(s), you'll notice that each one of your posts has a root style or theme that falls under one or more of the four categories on the next page...

It's helpful to know which type of post we tend to use most and get better at using the other three. Why? Because we must be continually alternating the way we engage with our audience.

Think of social media like a party.

For example, if you're constantly trying to EDUCATE everyone, you're the know-it-all at the party. Or, if you're constantly PROMOTING YOURSELF, you're the pushy saleswoman at the party.

Reminder: marketing is simply conversation.

Mix it up!

Be the woman at the party who shares funny and inspirational stories, as well as facts, and speaks highly of other local business owners. You still want to share facts from time to time, but do it in no more than one-quarter of your posts.

By coming up with diverse conversation topics, you are promoting yourself and your business without saying, "BUY NOW!". This is called providing the natural next steps, a natural progression rather than a HARD SELL.

☐ ACTION STEP #1

Look back at your last 20 posts on Facebook and/or Instagram. Write a checkmark in each box for every post that falls under that category. Notice which type of post you've been using most often.

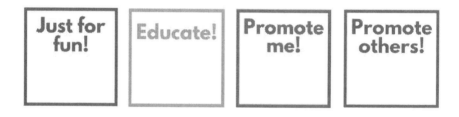

How I discovered the magic of storytelling…

I started writing this book on my 37th birthday in August, 2019. I rented a little rustic cabin as my own private writing retreat near Salmon Arm, BC. As I sat in front of my computer, watching rain drip off the roof, I thought back to where I was two years prior. I remember the exact day and exactly how I felt, what I was excited and worried about.

Two years before my writing retreat, on my 35th birthday, I was in Vernon, BC with son. I had just posted this on Facebook:

The summer I turned 35 was the first summer I had taken completely off of work. I had just written my first book, Money & The 39 Forever Mom, and my financial consulting business was three and a half years old. I felt I had come to a point in my life where I had earned a "selfish summer", or at least that was what I started out believing. By the end of that it, I realized my selfish summer had a huge impact on not only my career, but on my social media community: my clients and friends.

The marketing magic that happened was a result of sharing my stories, both stories from the past and what I was up to during my selfish summer.

I knew it was time to start sharing more of my life with my audience. I felt a shift, like I had taken a few steps up on my success ladder. I realized the podcasts and audiobooks were paying off. The way I invested my time and energy had changed and I was feeling the positive results of my perseverance. I decided it was time to celebrate and be done with worrying that my clients might think I was a slacker because I posted photos of me doing fun things too often.

Day after day, I was having fun in beautiful places, which meant I had original and eye-catching content daily: camping, horseback riding, eating ice cream and sea kayaking.

Although I didn't realize it until many months later, the marketing stars aligned for me during my selfish summer: timing, personal stories, the courage to open up about the toughest times in my life, and photos and videos in beautiful places.

The marketing magic I stumbled upon was simply sharing four types of stories over and over:

1. Share what you love, what matters most to you, or simply your favourite things to do and why.

2. Explain why you are grateful - for your amazing clients who believe in you enough to choose to work with you, for your health, for the beauty of the earth, for your wonderful family.

3. Share the stories of when life was harder for you and you were still figuring things out. Celebrate the struggles you faced that led your to your purpose.

4. Document your life. Share what you're up to right now.

Add pictures and videos, and voilà, marketing magic!

At first, I felt like I was bragging. I wasn't used to celebrating openly. I had to remind myself over and over again:

I'm not bragging. I'm fulfilling my purpose: inspire others to think bigger, be more and do more.

Another course correction…

As I continued to share my message of, *"When you work hard with a specific lifestyle in mind, an end goal, you can achieve it"*, I realized my original end goal of enjoying a "selfish summer" wasn't what I wanted. It was like serving the wrong clients: you have to do it for a while to understand you want to go in a different direction.

From "selfish summer" to summer camp.

My selfish summer began with five days of volunteering at a summer camp. I went to summer camp as a child and my cabin (or teepee) leaders had a huge impact on my life. I wanted to provide that experience for young girls once I was an adult, but I was too busy partying until I had my son at age 24 then spent the next ten years working to become financially stable.

As I came to the end of my selfish summer, I looked back at where it had began: at summer camp. I knew that's what I wanted to do with the majority of my summer the following year.

Summer 2020 will be my third year volunteering at Rivers Edge Camp. I'm there for about half the summer. The reward I get from that and the feeling my clients get from knowing that they support someone who gives back is the result I was looking for. I don't regret my selfish summer, just like I don't regret any of the "mistakes" I made on my journey to discovering my purpose.

☐ ACTION STEP #2

Some of your most powerful stories are buried deep or you may not realize how powerful they are. It's time to get to work writing down the *stories* behind the most valuable lessons you ever learned, the stuff that makes you YOU.

For this exercise, use your Facebook or Instagram profile to help you, if you've been posting about your life for more than a year. Look back on where you were 1, 3, 5 years ago and let the photos remind you of your greatest challenges, influential people and pinch me moments.

Write 3-5 stories for each question:

1. What **challenges** did you face that led you to finding more clarity or a better understanding of your purpose?

2. Who are the most **influential people** in your life and how did they make you a better person?

3. Describe your greatest **pinch me moments**; achievements, client success stories and dreams come true.

☐ ACTION STEP #3

In your partner meeting, share your favourite story from each topic by reading it aloud to her:

1.   Favourite Challenge

2.   Favourite Influential Person

3.   Favourite Pinch Me Moment

Then ask her which one was her favourite.

☐ ACTION STEP #4

Get your partner's help with choosing the best category for your favourite story, (there is no right or wrong answer) and write your story title in that box on the next page...

Categorize your stories:

Complete Action Step #5 with your partner if there is time, or on your own...

☐ ACTION STEP #5

Using the writing you did on the last three pages (or in your notebook), pick three more stories and put their titles in the appropriate boxes above.

If you're feeling called to share one of these stories right now, I encourage you to grab your phone, open your camera app and use my favourite method of sharing stories:

VIDEO!

If the thought of posting a video of you telling a story freaks you out, take some deep breaths. We'll get you there!

This isn't about you.

If it seems too big and bold for you to share stories about your life on social media, you need to reconnect with your purpose. This isn't about you. Your purpose is to serve others. Push the concerns of being judged or not being perfect out of your mind.

Speaking of video and not being perfect, I recently launched a video course called "Own Your Purpose". I loved building and sharing this course because it is about one of my favourite things: ***creating and editing video.***

I had no trouble building the material. The concepts I wanted to share flowed naturally from my pen to my notebook, then into a presentation at Canva.com. I was so excited to share my video knowledge, my number one passion, with a group of ladies.

As I shared my presentation on Zoom, I felt so excited. The women seemed engaged and I got some great information from them on what they believed to be true about the effectiveness of video and what was holding them back from creating more videos. When I got to the tech part of the course, which included a tour of my online video editing app and the features, I sensed a bit of confusion. Overall, however, I felt I had done a great job.

Later that day, I messaged all the attendees on Facebook asking for feedback and recommendations on how I could improve. The feedback was an even mix of, *"you nailed it"* and, *"you overwhelmed me and totally lost me a few times."*

Although they appreciated my enthusiastic attempt to share my video knowledge, I got the feeling I could have organized and delivered it more effectively.

I was quite impressed with my reaction to the negative feedback, I must say, which was reciting something I heard Rachel Hollis say,

Figure out what your audience likes by putting out "good enough" and getting feedback.

Speaking of feedback, I could really use your feedback! Please take five minutes to complete the survey about what you think of Fempreneur Marketing School and this book at **fempreneurmarketing.com/findyourvoicesurvey**. There's a free gift ($139 value) waiting for you at the end of the survey!

If you suck at writing and making videos and you feel completely frozen with fear at the thought of posting your stories on social media in written or video format, here's something else I heard Rachel Hollis say:

They will not remember that you posted, they will remember that you cared.

The thing that matters most when you are typing up a story or recording a video is WHY YOU'RE DOING IT.

Sure, there are other things that matter, like spelling and grammar. In a video, sound and lighting matter, but nothing matters as much as the reason why you're sharing that story, and that's what your audience will remember. If you are sharing because you care about improving lives, your spelling, grammar, lighting and sound will improve as long as you have a team giving you honest feedback.

Be a solid teammate.

I want to emphasize the need for your team and your partner as you begin sharing your stories. Remember, you gotta give to get, so you need to be there for your teammates, cheering them on and setting aside time to add value to their lives. Most women feel extremely raw and exposed as they begin to open up about things they have never shared with the world before. Encourage your teammates. Send a quick text or voice note saying how their story touched you. Like and comment on their posts. Your support will have a huge impact on your teammates, more than you may ever know.

☐ ACTION STEP #6

Offer the natural next steps to your audience by adding a "natural next step" to the end of each of your stories. Just like you did earlier in this chapter, write your story title in the appropriate box, then draw a line connecting the story with one of the natural next steps. (The ending for your "Promote Others" story will encourage your followers to like/follow your Fempreneur partner on social media.)

Tip: write a new hook using the instructions in the "Conversation" chapter, one that doesn't mention a survey, and add it as the ending to your "Promote Me" story!

☐ ACTION STEP #7

Write about the improvements you have made happen in your life in the last four weeks (mindset shifts, new ideas, new connections, new plans):

Reminder: add a few of your latest accomplishments to your goal board and immediately check them off!

☐ ACTION STEP #8

It's time to update your survey based on the feedback you received from your team and send it to 20 people. If you have a business or lead an organization, make sure no more than 10 of them are existing clients/

supporters. You will be amazed at how this act of asking for their opinion will WOW them and lead to new clients, customers and supporters!

The tech instructions on how to make changes to your survey are in a video at femporeneurmarketing.com/week4.

SHOW OFF YOUR SUCCESS!

Once you've completed all the action steps from this week and met with your partner, print and add the STORYTELLING BADGE to your goal board! Find it at femporeneurmarketing.com/week4.

4.
STORYTELLING
Chapter Summary

- People who relate to your stories will want to learn more about you. Provide the "natural next steps": <u>Contact Me</u>, <u>Buy Now</u> and <u>Learn More</u> (free ebook in exchange for email address).

- Celebrating your accomplishments openly will inspire others to think bigger, be more and do more. It's not bragging if your heart is in the right place.

- Share the stories behind the most valuable lessons you ever learned from challenges, influential people and pinch me moments.

- You may feel extremely raw and exposed as you begin to open up on social media, as will your teammates. Encourage one another. Send a quick text or voice note saying how their story touched you. Like and comment on each other's posts. Your support will have a huge impact on your teammates, more than you may ever know.

- Figure out what your audience likes by putting out 'good enough' and getting feedback.

- Your audience will not remember that you posted. They will remember that you cared.

- If you're feeling called to share one of your stories right now, grab your phone, open your camera app, prop your phone up against a glass of water and record a VIDEO of you sharing your story!

- *"Learn how to find beauty in your brokenness."*
  - Cynthia Hamilton Urquhart

Although you're arriving at the "Create" chapter just now, you've already created some really important, valuable things! You should be so proud of yourself!

NOTE: If you want to learn how to create ebooks to share your knowledge and build your email list, check this out:

A Free Bonus Chapter: eBook Creation Guide
at <u>fempreneurmarketing.com/create</u>.

<u>Complete the Action Steps in this chapter of the book prior to creating your eBook.</u>

☐ ACTION STEP #1

Check off everything you've created so far:

☐ Dream Team
☐ Fempreneur Partnership

☐ SMASH LIST
☐ My value statement

☐ Hook   ☐ Online Survey

☐ A description of my niche   ☐ My 9 most impactful stories

☐ Goal Board

If you created any of the following, put checks beside them, too:

☐ Facebook Business Page

☐ Instagram Business Profile

☐ Email gathering system (mailchimp.com)

☐ A video

Congratulations!

What else have you created over the past four weeks? Write more creations in the space above and CELEBRATE by rewarding yourself with something special (that you can afford). I know how hard you've worked to push through the fear, excuses and distractions while you've been making positive change happen. You've done an incredible job of showing up for yourself and those you serve! *Celebrate and reward yourself!*

An important part of finding your voice on social media is putting your message in visual format.

You and your partner will need to give each other a little extra support this week as you learn how to use a new tech tool to create beautiful, eye-catching images. By the way, it's normal to want to punch your computer in the face a few times as you learn how to bring your ideas to life!

This week, your partner is going to create images to help you find your voice on social media. You are going to do the same for her.

NOTE: Step-by-step instructions are in a video at fempreneurmarketing.com/week5.

☐ ACTION STEP #1

Create <u>three</u> images for your partner at <u>canva.com</u>, a free online tool for creating beautiful images, presentations and more!

Create one image for each purpose:

• Just for fun   • Educate   • Promote

Use this list for inspiration of what to say on the images:

- quotes from her stories
- quotes from others that bolster her cause/message
- words of wisdom (smart things you've heard her say that will be helpful to others)
- an event invite including the event name, date, time, location and the link to get tickets/RSVP
- an advertisement for her product or service (include her website)

Create images that will speak to her niche, the specific people she is trying to reach on social media.

A few months after I launched Fempreneur Marketing School, I attended a group therapy session with horses led by Amy Monea and Angie Payne. Before we went into the arena with the horses, we sat in a circle and Angie led us through a meditation. The meditation changed my life.

☐ ACTION STEP #2

During your meeting with your partner, listen to the mediation at fempreneurmarketing.com/week5. Make sure you are in a place that is quiet. Once the meditation is over, write every detail of what you saw and felt in the space below:

☐ ACTION STEP #3

Create at least <u>four</u> images for yourself, one for each of your stories, at canva.com:

When creating your images, stay focused on your purpose. When you get frustrated (you will, I guarantee it!), use the meditation in Action Step #2.

☐ ACTION STEP #4

Create a fifth image: for your survey. I recommend you use your professional headshot or a photo of you with space for text on one side of your face/body. Say something like, *"How can I best serve you?"* or, *"May I have your opinion?"*

You must share photos of **YOU** on your social media channels! Posting only stock images of scenery, food, sports, fashion, etc. will not engage your audience, nor will photos you take of activities and places if the photos don't include your face.

At least one in every ten images you share should feature the messenger: YOU.

Getting comfortable taking photos and videos of yourself, whether by selfies or using the glass of water technique, is a necessary part of finding your voice. People are visual. We need to see who the message is coming from.

Tip: *I prefer to use a tall glass of water to prop up my phone. I rarely use a tripod and I don't own a selfie stick.*

If you don't have a professional headshot image that was taken in the last three years, the next Action Step is very important...

□ ACTION STEP #5

If you haven't had a professional headshot taken in the last three years, hire a photographer to take your photo. Investing in a professional headshot will repay you ten-fold when you use it on your social media images, invites to events, business card, LinkedIn profile and brochures/ flyers. It is also a great idea to have 5-10 photos of you in action - doing what you do - with your clients. Ask your favourite client if she is willing to pose in a photo shoot for marketing purposes.

If you live in the Calgary area, my friend and photographer, Lisa Henry, can help you out with that photo shoot.

Meet Lisa…

Five years ago, I fell in love with photography. It was the creative outlet I had been looking for for a long time. At the time, I was a stay at home mom and I was looking for something outside of mommyhood to remind me of who I was. Don't get me wrong, I LOVE being a mom and I am so thankful I get to stay home with my children, but I did feel a pull for more.

I started my business, Lisa Gabriel Photography, in 2016 and have been slowly growing it ever since. Along my business building journey, my husband has asked me numerous times what success looks like to me and I never knew the answer. I knew I loved taking photos of people that capture their authentic beauty. I love being able to freeze moments in time so people can enjoy them forever.

In 2018, I joined Lyndsie's "Mompreneur" group which later became the "Fempreneurs". I have learned so much about business and myself through the women in this community. The knowledge support couldn't have come at a better time, as I prepared to dive deeper into growing my business.

In September 2019, my youngest started kindergarten and I was so excited for the time I could focus on my business. Instead, to my surprise, I felt unmotivated and depressed in this new stage of life. I had gone from being a university student directly into motherhood and I didn't know what it meant to be "Lisa The Adult", I just knew how to be "Mom". I started talking about how I was feeling with some other mothers who had older kids and they understood what I was talking about. They told me to take some time to find myself, to give myself grace in this transition phase.

A few weeks later, I woke up on a Monday morning with a clear plan for what success was going to look like for me: to build and grow my business so I can hire, train and help other stay at home moms earn money and have something to remind them of who they are outside of "Mom".

I am telling you this story because I want to spread the good news that took me years to discover:

Fulfilling, profitable work <u>can</u> be done within the bounds of a stay at home mom life.

There is nothing like being part of a supportive community of women who are starting and growing businesses, many of which are also moms. That's why I'm so grateful for the YYC Fempreneurs.

It may have taken me longer than I'd like to "find myself", but I know I have finally found my purpose. I know I needed everything that has happened since I became a mom to get me here. I am really excited for all that is to come!

"Don't rush finding your purpose. It will find you when the time is right."
- Lisa Henry

☐ ACTION STEP #6

Share your survey either publicly or with a specific group of people. If you have a job, for example, you may not want your boss to know that you are starting a "side hustle". Use your discretion with this step. It isn't right for everyone. An alternative to sharing your survey publicly is emailing it to a select group of people. Put in the body of the email:

- Survey image
- Hook wording
- Survey link

☐ ACTION STEP #7

What else do you want to create? Make a list below and put your top priority creation on your goal board.

Reminder: Grad Night is less than two weeks away! If your team leader hasn't created an image with the location and details of your Grad Night yet, let her know you'd like to do it and head to <u>canva.com</u>!

5.
CREATE
Chapter Summary

- An important part of finding your voice on social media is putting your message in visual format.

- My go-to (free) tool for creating eye-catching images, presentations and more is canva.com.

- You are guaranteed to feel frustrated when you're new to using canva.com. Push through the frustration by focusing on your purpose to serve others.

- Use the meditation at fempreneurmarketing.com/week5 to refocus on your purpose and your goals.

- Don't post only stock photos or photos of scenery and things that don't include you. At least one in every ten images you post should feature the messenger: YOU.

- If you haven't had a professional headshot taken in the last three years, it's time to invest in one.

- *"Don't rush finding your purpose. It will find you when the time is right."* - Lisa Henry

Welcome to your final week in Fempreneur Marketing School!

This chapter is about building systems and processes that will help you continue to create, achieve, celebrate and repeat!

Automating areas of your business is like automating your monthly savings and bill payments. You know the stuff you need to do every week or month without fail in your business, so why not save time by automating them?

Set it and forget it.

Meet my friend, automation expert and personal trainer, Liz...

When I learned about the four types of social media posts: just for fun, educate, promote me and promote others, I was blown away. Social media couldn't be THAT easy, could it? Finding that out gave me the clarity and inspiration I needed to build lists of different types of posts.

When I was introduced to the concept of "batching" my social media posts, meaning creating and scheduling my week's posts every Sunday, I was thrilled! For the longest time, my greatest challenge was coming up with stuff to post on social media, and not just "stuff" but valuable, helpful information. I had doubts all the time about "is this a good post?", and would quickly shut it down and not post at all because of the doubts I had.

Then came the real game-changer: a little gem called "Creator Studio".

Creator Studio is a *FREE* tool that allows you to plan and schedule your social media posts on Facebook and Instagram, and you can find it at <u>facebook.com/creatorstudio</u>. You simply upload your images, videos, and text (including hashtags) and then schedule the day and time you want each post to happen.

Since discovering this "batching" system a year ago, I have been setting aside two hours every Sunday to create and schedule my posts.

Lyndsie asked me to share with you the number one thing I learned in Fempreneur Marketing School. It is most definitely the concept of planning my social media posts ahead of time so I can spend less time on my phone. My schedule is crammed as it is and Creator Studio has been a real lifesaver. When an idea for something to post comes to me during the week, I "schedule it in"/put it in my Google calendar for Sunday. Every Sunday, I make and schedule my social posts for the next seven days. Depending on how much the creative juices are flowing, it takes me anywhere from an hour to an hour and a half to schedule a full week's worth of content, then I don't have to worry about it!

Before using this system, I felt overwhelmed and scatter-brained because I felt the need to post SOMETHING regardless of if I had a good idea or not. Knowing I have time set aside to plan and schedule my posts takes the stress off and actually helps me be more creative.

The second most important thing I gained from Fempreneur Marketing School (this is actually tied for first place but Lyndsie has talked about this a lot in this book already!) is the women I've met in the YYC Fempreneur Community. I love meeting the new marketing school grads at grad night celebrations. They're all such amazing, talented women who love supporting one another. It feels great to know your social media posts are going out to a community that supports you and wants you to succeed. You can go to them for advice and their input is always coming from a place of love. The likes and comments I get on my posts from other members of this community always make me smile, and many of the women have supported me by participating in my group fitness classes both live and online.

When it comes to automation, it's not just important to automate technology. Your weekly meetings with your Fempreneur partner are just as important. You need that time with someone who really gets you and wants to help you succeed, someone who can give you a gentle push towards your goal. Everything you attempt to build will turn out better if you do it with your partner and team alongside you.

Don't stop meeting with your partner at the end of week six. I still meet with my partner to catch up and see how she's doing, and I know she's interested in what I have going on, too. Prioritize those meetings just like you're setting aside time to plan your social media posts. Set aside time at least every other week to work on your businesses and celebrate wins as a team.

Lastly, because I'm a personal trainer, I want to encourage you to prioritize your health and fitness. Set aside time each day to nourish your body with healthy food and to strengthen and lengthen your body with exercise. If you need help with finding a nutrition and/or exercise plan that's right for you, including meal planning, get in touch with me!

It's such a gift to be able to make money doing something we love, but the freedom to do what we want when we want can actually get in the way of our success. You will need to build boundaries around your time and energy. Although I don't believe a person can ever find a perfect balance, especially as a business owner, I hope what I've *shared here will help you automate your social media posts, prioritize meetings with your teammates and take better care of yourself so you can feel healthy and vibrant <u>most</u> of the time.*

"Strive for progress, not perfection!"
- Liz Campbell

☐ ACTION STEP #1

During your partner meeting, take turns planning each other's next seven days of social media posts in your notebook. Decide if you are going to post once or twice a day and create either seven or fourteen posts. Incorporate your writing you did in the "Storytelling" chapter. Aim to build an equal number of each type of post:

- Just for fun
- Educate

- Promote Me
- Promote Others

Use one or two of your partner's posts (with her permission) for "Promote Others" and be sure to promote a few of your favourite local businesses.

☐ ACTION STEP #2

Dedicate a three hour time block to work on your business this week. This time block needs to happen <u>after</u> your partner meeting as you will need your completed social media plan.

During your three hour time block, you will create and schedule your posts. This might take more than three hours the first time, but once you do this a few times, you'll have it down to less than two hours, especially if you use the **Automation Agenda:**

- Create an image for each post at <u>canva.com</u> or simply take photos with your phone, email them to yourself and download them to your computer. For examples of the types of images to create/shoot, scroll through a few of your favourite profiles on Instagram and/or Facebook.

- Type the post text in Google Docs for each post at <u>google.com/document</u>.

- Choose one or two of your stories/messages that you feel inspired to share in a video. BE BRAVE! YOU CAN DO THIS! Just like with the photos, email the videos to yourself from your phone and download them to your computer.

- Write on paper the date and time you want each post to happen. Keep the sheet of paper on your desk next to your keyboard.

- On your computer, go to www.facebook.com/creatorstudio and get to work scheduling your posts! If you have trouble with this, Google it and watch a how-to video or read a blog from one of the world's many helpful social media gurus. You will also find information and tips at fempreneurmarketing.com/week6.

Make time in your life for the things that are important to you.

Setting aside two or three hours once a week for the foreseeable future will be challenging. You will have to put your clients first. You will have to say no to cleaning the bathroom today or to lunch with friends sometimes.

Automation is about making room for what's important, but sometimes we need help with this. Sometimes the simple solution is right in front of us, but we can't see it.

Meet my friend and trained professional organizer, Mélanie Higuchi...

My journey to becoming a solo-preneur was an unintended one. Before starting my business, I was the office manager at a naturopath clinic. At the time, I felt that my path in life was set out in front of me: work at the clinic until I retire. However, the universe had a different plan for me.

In 2013, I was hit with a massive curve-ball that would change my life path trajectory forever. I was diagnosed with Chronic Lyme disease. In the coming months I was in bed, not able to do much of anything due to extreme fatigue, pain and neurological dysfunction. Having been sick for most of my life (not knowing I had Lyme), I have always tried to find the life lesson in my challenges.

As I layed in bed and considered my options, I realized my returning to working at the clinic may not be the best option, or what I was meant to do. Upon reflection, the part I loved most about myself (and was really good at) was my ability to organize, a skill I used daily at my office manager job. It brought me so much joy to give others that feeling of, "a weight has been lifted" when I organized a space for them. I had discovered my greatest gift and source of joy by organizing friends' closets and kitchen pantries! Although I loved my job at the clinic, the thing I loved most about it was something I could do anywhere: ORGANIZE!

My research into the world of organizing as a career and the powerful impact my skills could have on people led me to starting the business I own and operate today, Functional Spaces.

When people are in the thick of disorganization, something that happens to all of us, we often don't keep the bigger picture in mind. We lose sight of our vision and goals. When people know what they want, they search for ways to get there faster and with ease. They try to make room for what's important to them, but sometimes, they can't see the solution clearly.

When I was the office manager at the naturopath clinic, I observed the ways each practitioner went about their day. I noticed that on many occasions, they were leaving the treatment room to grab missing supplies. I made notes of where the ideal location would be for each form, medical instrument and other supplies.

One weekend, I went to the clinic when no one was there. I put my streamlining systems in place, making sure everything was easy to find. My goal was not only to bring joy to my co-workers, but also to give the patients more time with their practitioners.

On Monday, I was known as the "organizing gnome". It was like magic had happened! I loved the feeling of knowing I had made a positive impact on their lives. My simple, yet effective changes allowed them to feel more at ease, more professional (less leaving the room to grab supplies) and more organized.

My organizing approach is simple: determine what you want in life, just like in the "Purpose" chapter of this book. Write down what you want to achieve, your visions and goals. Then organize your home and office with that in mind. Being more organized will ultimately help you to keep room in your life for what truly matters.

If you are struggling to achieve your goals, or are weighed down from the stress of the stuff around you, reach out for help! This could be from a friend, family member or even a professional like myself.

Now that I have my own business, I help many clients with all sorts of organizational needs. I take great pride in knowing I am helping them move past the shame of being disorganized to ultimately reaching their goal of living a simpler and more fulfilled life. I am thankful for their vulnerability and give them huge credit for asking for help.

Mélanie Higuchi
www.functionalspaces.ca
f /functionalspaces

"The hardest part of improving isn't doing the work, it's asking for help."
- Mélanie Higuchi

☐ ACTION STEP #3

Schedule a three hour time block every week for the next three months to plan and schedule your social media posts.

6.
AUTOMATE
Chapter Summary

- Automating areas of your business is like automating your monthly savings and bill payments.

- Plan and schedule your social media posts during a specific time block on one day each and every week.

- When planning your social media posts, aim to build an equal number of each type: just for fun, educate, promote me, promote others.

- *"Strive for progress, not perfection."* - Liz Campbell

- Sometimes the simple solution is right in front of us, but we can't see it.

- *"The hardest part of improving isn't doing the work, it's asking for help."* - Mélanie Higuchi

For six weeks, you've worked hard to make the changes necessary to have a big impact on this world. This calls for a celebration!

It's time to create a fun and exciting evening where your teammates as well as other women in your community can build real connections. Treat this event like a birthday party for all the women on your team and ask them to invite a few female friends who want to cheer them on and celebrate their success. Make it BIG! Keep track of who's attending by creating a Facebook event (make sure you have a big enough section reserved if you plan to hold grad night at a restaurant.)

☐ Party Planning Item #1: PRIZES

Ask each member of your group to donate a prize or two, such as products or gift cards. This is also a great opportunity for the business owners on your team to promote their businesses by offering a free gift or coupon.

Award the donated prizes one of two ways:

- "Swag bags", where each team member gets a bag full of the same stuff
- Each person gets a different prize

I usually pick up one or two of my favourite books (Dale Carnegie, Tim Ferriss, Pat Flynn) and give those as the "big prizes" and raffle them off throughout the evening.

The next party planning item is the game you will play to award the prizes...

☐ Party Planning Item #2: GAME

Bring to the party enough for everyone:

- pens
- recipe cards or small squares of paper

You will also need a bucket, bowl or pitcher to draw the folded pieces of paper from.

Each teammate will write on their recipe card:

1. Their name
2. The biggest and most impactful change or mindset shift they gained from Fempreneur Marketing School

Put all the pieces of paper in the bucket/bowl and draw them one at a time. When someone's name is drawn, she shares aloud her name, her business or business idea or reason for joining Fempreneur Marketing School, and then shares what she wrote on her card.

Every time someone shares out loud, we hoot and holler and clap for her. excitedly!!!

☐ Party Planning Item #3: TEAM PHOTO

Do this before awarding the prizes!

Please tag **@yycfempreneurs** when you post your team photo!

REFERENCE GUIDE

BONUS GIFTS

To help you continually up your game, I've created a FREE mini ebook series for you!

**All the tools in this book are available in a
FREE mini ebook series at
<u>fempreneurmarketing.com/tools</u>.**

I also have a surprise free gift for you in exchange for your feedback on this book and Fempreneur Marketing School. The survey and your surprise free gift are at:
<u>fempreneurmarketing.com/findyourvoicesurvey</u>.

Thank you for reading this book and for supporting other women!

Lyndsie Barrie

Manufactured by Amazon.ca
Bolton, ON